THE PELICAN SHAKESPEARE
GENERAL EDITORS

STEPHEN ORGEL
A. R. BRAUNMULLER

The First Part of
King Henry the Fourth

J. H. Hackett as Falstaff, c. 1850

William Shakespeare

The First Part of
King Henry the Fourth

EDITED BY CLAIRE MCEACHERN

PENGUIN BOOKS

PENGUIN BOOKS
Published by the Penguin Group
Penguin Group (USA) Inc., 375 Hudson Street, New York, New York 10014, U.S.A.
Penguin Group (Canada), 90 Eglinton Avenue East, Suite 700, Toronto,
Ontario, Canada M4P 2Y3 (a division of Pearson Penguin Canada Inc.)
Penguin Books Ltd, 80 Strand, London WC2R 0RL, England
Penguin Ireland, 25 St Stephen's Green, Dublin 2, Ireland (a division of Penguin Books Ltd)
Penguin Group (Australia), 250 Camberwell Road, Camberwell,
Victoria 3124, Australia (a division of Pearson Australia Group Pty Ltd)
Penguin Books India Pvt Ltd, 11 Community Centre, Panchsheel Park,
New Delhi – 110 017, India
Penguin Group (NZ), 67 Apollo Drive, Rosedale, North Shore 0632, New Zealand
(a division of Pearson New Zealand Ltd)
Penguin Books (South Africa) (Pty) Ltd, 24 Sturdee Avenue, Rosebank,
Johannesburg 2196, South Africa

Penguin Books Ltd, Registered Offices: 80 Strand, London WC2R 0RL, England

The First Part of King Henry the Fourth edited by M. A. Shaaber
published in the United States of America in Penguin Books 1957
Revised edition published 1970
This new edition edited by Claire McEachern published 2000

20 19

Copyright © Penguin Books Inc., 1957, 1970
Copyright © Penguin Putnam Inc., 2000
All rights reserved

ISBN 978-0-14-071456-2

Printed in the United States of America
Set in Garamond
Designed by Virginia Norey

Contents

Publisher's Note

IT IS ALMOST half a century since the first volumes of the
Pelican Shakespeare appeared under the general editorship
of Alfred Harbage. The fact that a new edition, rather
than simply a revision, has been undertaken reflects the
profound changes textual and critical studies of Shakespeare have undergone in the past twenty years. For the
new Pelican series, the texts of the plays and poems have
been thoroughly revised in accordance with recent schol-
arship, and in some cases have been entirely reedited. New
introductions and notes have been provided in all the volumes. But the new Shakespeare is also designed as a suc-
cessor to the original series; the previous editions have
been taken into account, and the advice of the previous
editors has been solicited where it was feasible to do so.

Certain textual features of the new Pelican Shakespeare
should be particularly noted. All lines are numbered that
contain a word, phrase, or allusion explained in the
glossarial notes. In addition, for convenience, every tenth
line is also numbered, in italics when no annotation is indicated. The intrusive and often inaccurate place headings
inserted by early editors are omitted (as is becoming standard practice), but for the convenience of those who miss
them, an indication of locale now appears as the first item
in the annotation of each scene.

In the interest of both elegance and utility, each speech
prefix is set in a separate line when the speaker's lines are
in verse, except when those words form the second half of
a verse line. Thus the verse form of the speech is kept vi-
sually intact. What is printed as verse and what is printed
as prose has, in general, the authority of the original texts.
Departures from the original texts in this regard have only
the authority of editorial tradition and the judgment of
the Pelican editors; and, in a few instances, are admittedly
arbitrary.

The Theatrical World

Economic realities determined the theatrical world in which Shakespeare's plays were written, performed, and received. For centuries in England, the primary theatrical tradition was nonprofessional. Craft guilds (or "mysteries") provided religious drama – mystery plays – as part of the celebration of religious and civic festivals, and schools and universities staged classical and neoclassical drama in both Latin and English as part of their curricula. In these forms, drama was established and socially acceptable. Professional theater, in contrast, existed on the margins of society. The acting companies were itinerant; playhouses could be any available space – the great halls of the aristocracy, town squares, civic halls, inn yards, fair booths, or open fields – and income was sporadic, dependent on the passing of the hat or on the bounty of local patrons. The actors, moreover, were considered little better than vagabonds, constantly in danger of arrest or expulsion.

In the late 1560s and 1570s, however, English professional theater began to gain respectability. Wealthy aristocrats fond of drama – the Lord Admiral, for example, or the Lord Chamberlain – took acting companies under their protection so that the players technically became members of their households and were no longer subject to arrest as homeless or masterless men. Permanent theaters were first built at this time as well, allowing the companies to control and charge for entry to their performances.

Shakespeare's livelihood, and the stunning artistic explosion in which he participated, depended on pragmatic and architectural effort. Professional theater requires ways to restrict access to its offerings; if it does not, and admission fees cannot be charged, the actors do not get paid, the costumes go to a pawnbroker, and there is no such thing as a professional, ongoing theatrical tradition. The answer to that economic need arrived in the late 1560s and 1570s with the creation of the so-called public or amphitheater playhouse. Recent discoveries indicate that the precursor of the Globe playhouse in London (where Shakespeare's mature plays were presented) and the Rose theater (which presented Christopher Marlowe's plays and some of Shakespeare's earliest ones) was the Red Lion theater of 1567. Archaeological studies of the foundations of the Rose and Globe theaters have revealed that the open-air theater of the 1590s and later was probably a polygonal building with fourteen to twenty or twenty-four sides, multistoried, from 75 to 100 feet in diameter, with a raised, partly covered "thrust" stage that projected into a group of standing patrons, or "groundlings," and a covered gallery, seating up to 2,500 or more (very crowded) spectators.

These theaters might have been about half full on any given day, though the audiences were larger on holidays or when a play was advertised, as old and new were, through printed playbills posted around London. The metropolitan area's late-Tudor, early-Stuart population (circa 1590-1620) has been estimated at about 150,000 to 250,000. It has been supposed that in the mid-1590s there were about 15,000 spectators per week at the public theaters; thus, as many as 10 percent of the local population went to the theater regularly. Consequently, the theaters' repertories – the plays available for this experienced and frequent audience – had to change often: in the month between September 15 and October 15, 1595, for instance, the Lord Admiral's Men performed twenty-eight times in eighteen different plays.

Since natural light illuminated the amphitheaters' stages, performances began between noon and two o'clock and ran without a break for two or three hours. They often concluded with a jig, a fencing display, or some other nondramatic exhibition. Weather conditions determined the season for the amphitheaters: plays were performed every day (including Sundays, sometimes, to clerical dismay) except during Lent – the forty days before Easter – or periods of plague, or sometimes during the summer months when law courts were not in session and the most affluent members of the audience were not in London.

To a modern theatergoer, an amphitheater stage like that of the Rose or Globe would appear an unfamiliar mixture of plainness and elaborate decoration. Much of the structure was carved or painted, sometimes to imitate marble; elsewhere, as under the canopy projecting over the stage, to represent the stars and the zodiac. Appropriate painted canvas pictures (of Jerusalem, for example, if the play was set in that city) were apparently hung on the wall behind the acting area, and tragedies were accompanied by black hangings, presumably something like crepe festoons or bunting. Although these theaters did not employ what we would call scenery, early modern spectators saw numerous large props, such as the "bar" at which a prisoner stood during a trial, the "mossy bank" where lovers reclined, an arbor for amorous conversation, a chariot, gallows, tables, trees, beds, thrones, writing desks, and so forth. Audiences might learn a scene's location from a sign (reading "Athens," for example) carried across the stage (as in Bertolt Brecht's twentieth-century productions). Equally captivating (and equally irritating to the theater's enemies) were the rich costumes and personal props the actors used: the most valuable items in the surviving theatrical inventories are the swords, gowns, robes, crowns, and other items worn or carried by the performers.

Magic appealed to Shakespeare's audiences as much as it does to us today, and the theater exploited many deceptive and spectacular devices. A winch in the loft above the stage, called "the heavens," could lower and raise actors playing gods, goddesses, and other supernatural figures to and from the main acting area, just as one or more trapdoors permitted entrances and exits to and from the area, called "hell," beneath the stage. Actors wore elementary makeup such as wigs, false beards, and face paint, and they employed pig's bladders filled with animal blood to make wounds seem more real. They had rudimentary but effective ways of pretending to behead or hang a person. Supernumeraries (stagehands or actors not needed in a particular scene) could make thunder sounds (by shaking a metal sheet or rolling an iron ball down a chute) and show lightning (by blowing inflammable resin through tubes into a flame). Elaborate fireworks enhanced the effects of dragons flying through the air or imitated such celestial phenomena as comets, shooting stars, and multiple suns. Horses' hoofbeats, bells (located perhaps in the tower above the stage), trumpets and drums, clocks, cannon shots and gunshots, and the like were common sound effects. And the music of viols, cornets, oboes, and recorders was a regular feature of theatrical performances.

For two relatively brief spans, from the late 1570s to 1590 and from 1599 to 1614, the amphitheaters competed with the so-called private, or indoor, theaters, which originated as, or later represented themselves as, educational institutions training boys as singers for church services and court performances. These indoor theaters had two features that were distinct from the amphitheaters': their personnel and their playing spaces. The amphitheaters' adult companies included both adult men, who played the male roles, and boys, who played the female roles; the private, or indoor, theater companies, on the other hand, were entirely composed of boys aged about 8 to 16, who were, or could pretend to be, candidates for singers in a church or a royal boys' choir. (Until 1660, professional theatrical companies included no women.) The playing space would appear much more familiar to modern audiences than the long-vanished amphitheaters; the later indoor theaters were, in fact, the ancestors of the typical modern theater. They were enclosed spaces, usually rectangular, with the stage filling one end of the rectangle and the audience arrayed in seats or benches across (and sometimes lining) the building's longer axis. These spaces staged plays less frequently than the public theaters (perhaps only once a week) and held far fewer spectators than the amphitheaters: about 200 to 600, as opposed to 2,500 or more. Fewer patrons mean a smaller gross income, unless each pays more. Not surprisingly, then, private theaters charged higher prices than the amphitheaters, probably sixpence, as opposed to a penny for the cheapest entry.

Protected from the weather, the indoor theaters presented plays later in the day than the amphitheaters, and used artificial illumination – candles in sconces or candelabra. But candles melt, and need replacing, snuffing, and trimming, and these practical requirements may have been part of the reason the indoor theaters introduced breaks in the performance, the intermission so dear to the heart of theatergoers and to the pocketbooks of theater concessionaires ever since. Whether motivated by the need to tend to the candles or by the entrepreneurs' wishing to sell oranges and liquor, or both, the indoor theaters eventually established the modern convention of the non-continuous performance. In the early modern "private" theater, musical performances apparently filled the intermissions, which in Stuart theater jargon seem to have been called "acts."

At the end of the first decade of the seventeenth century, the distinction between public amphitheaters and private indoor companies ceased. For various cultural, political, and economic reasons, individual companies gained control of both the public, open-air theaters and the indoor ones, and companies mixing adult men and boys took over the formerly "private" theaters. Despite the death of the boys' companies and of their highly innovative theaters (for which such luminous playwrights as Ben Jonson, George Chapman, and John Marston wrote), their playing spaces and conventions had an immense impact on subsequent plays: not merely for the intervals (which stressed the artistic and architectonic importance of "acts"), but also because they introduced political and social satire as a popular dramatic ingredient, even in tragedy, and a wider range of actorly effects, encouraged by their more intimate playing spaces.

Even the briefest sketch of the Shakespearean theatrical world would be incomplete without some comment on the social and cultural dimensions of theaters and playing in the period. In an intensely hierarchical and status-conscious society, professional actors and their ventures had hardly any respectability; as we have indicated, to protect themselves against laws designed to curb vagabondage and the increase of masterless men, actors resorted to the near-fiction that they were the servants of noble masters, and wore their distinctive livery. Hence the company for which Shakespeare wrote in the 1590s called itself the Lord Chamberlain's Men and pretended that the public, money-getting performances were in fact rehearsals for private performances before that high court official. From 1598, the Privy Council had licensed theatrical companies, and after 1603, with the accession of King James I, the companies gained explicit royal protection, just as the Queen's Men had for a time under Queen Elizabeth. The Chamberlain's Men became the King's Men, and the other companies were patronized by the other members of the royal family.

These designations were legal fictions that half-concealed an important economic and social development, the evolution away from the theater's organization on the model of the guild, a self-regulating confraternity of individual artisans, into a proto-capitalist organization. Shakespeare's company became a joint-stock company, where persons who supplied capital and, in some cases, such as Shakespeare's, capital and talent, employed themselves and others in earning a return on that capital. This development meant that actors and theater companies were outside both the traditional guild structures, which required some form of civic or royal charter, and the feudal household organization of master-and-servant. This anomalous, maverick social and economic condition made theater companies practically unruly and potentially even dangerous; consequently, numerous official bodies – including the London metropolitan and ecclesiastical authorities as well as, occasionally, the royal court itself – tried, without much success, to control and even to disband them.

Public officials had good reason to want to close the theaters: they were attractive nuisances – they drew often riotous crowds, they were always noisy, and they could be politically offensive and socially insubordinate. Until the Civil War, however, anti-theatrical forces failed to shut down professional theater, for many reasons – limited surveillance and few police powers, tensions or outright hostilities among the agencies that sought to check or channel theatrical activity, and lack of clear policies for control. Another reason must have been the theaters' undeniable popularity. Curtailing any activity enjoyed by such a substantial percentage of the population was difficult, as various Roman emperors attempting to limit circuses had learned, and the Tudor-Stuart audience was not merely large, it was socially diverse and included women. The prevalence of public entertainment in this period has been underestimated. In fact, fairs, holidays, games, sporting events, the equivalent of modern parades, freak shows, and street exhibitions all abounded, but the theater was the most widely and frequently available entertainment to which people of every class had access. That fact helps account both for its quantity and for the fear and anger it aroused.

WILLIAM SHAKESPEARE OF STRATFORD-UPON-AVON, GENTLEMAN

Many people have said that we know very little about William Shakespeare's life – pinheads and postcards are often mentioned as appropriately tiny surfaces on which to record the available information. More imaginatively and perhaps more correctly, Ralph Waldo Emerson wrote, "Shakespeare is the only biographer of Shakespeare. . . . So far from Shakespeare's being the least known, he is the one person in all modern history fully known to us."

In fact, we know more about Shakespeare's life than we do about almost any other English writer's of his era. His last will and testament (dated March 25, 1616) survives, as do numerous legal contracts and court documents involving Shakespeare as principal or witness, and parish records in Stratford and London. Shakespeare appears quite often in official records of King James's royal court, and of course Shakespeare's name appears on numerous title pages and in the written and recorded words of his literary contemporaries Robert Greene, Henry Chettle, Francis Meres, John Davies of Hereford, Ben Jonson, and many others. Indeed, if we make due allowance for the bloating of modern, run-of-the-mill bureaucratic records, more information has survived over the past four hundred years about William Shakespeare of Stratford-upon-Avon, Warwickshire, than is likely to survive in the next four hundred years about any reader of these words.

What we do not have are entire categories of information – Shakespeare's private letters or diaries, drafts and revisions of poems and plays, critical prefaces or essays, commendatory verse for other writers' works, or instructions guiding his fellow actors in their performances, for instance – that we imagine would help us understand and appreciate his surviving writings. For all we know, many such data never existed as written records. Many literary and theatrical critics, not knowing what might once have existed, more or less cheerfully accept the situation; some even make a theoretical virtue of it by claiming that such data are irrelevant to understanding and interpreting the plays and poems.

So, what do we know about William Shakespeare, the man responsible for thirty-seven or perhaps more plays, more than 150 sonnets, two lengthy narrative poems, and some shorter poems?

While many families by the name of Shakespeare (or some variant spelling) can be identified in the English Midlands as far back as the twelfth century, it seems likely that the dramatist's grandfather, Richard, moved to Snitterfield, a town not far from Stratford-upon-Avon, sometime before 1529. In Snitterfield, Richard Shakespeare leased farmland from the very wealthy Robert Arden. By 1552, Richard's son John had moved to a large house on Henley Street in Stratford-upon-Avon, the house that stands today as "The Birthplace." In Stratford, John Shakespeare traded as a glover, dealt in wool, and lent money at interest; he also served in a variety of civic posts, including "High Bailiff," the municipality's equivalent of mayor. In 1557, he married Robert Arden's youngest daughter, Mary. Mary and John had four sons – William was the oldest – and four daughters, of whom only Joan outlived her most celebrated sibling. William was baptized (an event entered in the Stratford parish church records) on April 26, 1564, and it has become customary, without any good factual support, to suppose he was born on April 23, which happens to be the feast day of Saint George, patron saint of England, and is also the date on which he died, in 1616. Shakespeare married Anne Hathaway in 1582, when he was eighteen and she was twenty-six; their first child was born five months later. It has been generally assumed that the marriage was enforced and subsequently unhappy, but these are only assumptions; it has been estimated, for instance, that up to one third of Elizabethan brides were pregnant when they married. Anne and William Shakespeare had three children: Susanna, who married a prominent local physician, John Hall; and the twins Hamnet, who died young in 1596, and Judith, who married Thomas Quiney – apparently a rather shady individual. The name Hamnet was unusual but not unique: he and his twin sister were named for their godparents, Shakespeare's neighbors Hamnet and Judith Sadler. Shakespeare's father died in 1601 (the year of *Hamlet*), and Mary Arden Shakespeare died in 1608 (the year of *Coriolanus*). William Shakespeare's last surviving direct descendant was his granddaughter Elizabeth Hall, who died in 1670.

Between the birth of the twins in 1585 and a clear reference to Shakespeare as a practicing London dramatist in Robert Greene's sensationalizing, satiric pamphlet, *Greene's Groatsworth of Wit* (1592), there is no record of where William Shakespeare was or what he was doing. These seven so-called lost years have been imaginatively filled by scholars and other students of Shakespeare: some think he traveled to Italy, or fought in the Low Countries, or studied law or medicine, or worked as an apprentice actor/writer, and so on to even more fanciful possibilities. Whatever the biographical facts for those "lost" years, Greene's nasty remarks in 1592 testify to professional envy and to the fact that Shakespeare already had a successful career in London. Speaking to his fellow playwrights, Greene warns both generally and specifically:

> . . . trust them [actors] not: for there is an upstart crow, beautified with our feathers, that with his tiger's heart wrapped in a player's hide supposes he is as well able to bombast out a blank verse as the best of you; and being an absolute Johannes Factotum, is in his own conceit the only Shake-scene in a country.

The passage mimics a line from *3 Henry VI* (hence the play must have been performed before Greene wrote) and seems to say that "Shake-scene" is both actor and playwright, a jack-of-all-trades. That same year, Henry Chettle protested Greene's remarks in *Kind-Heart's Dream,* and each of the next two years saw the publication of poems – *Venus and Adonis* and *The Rape of Lucrece,* respectively – publicly ascribed to (and dedicated by) Shakespeare. Early in 1595 he was named as one of the senior members of a prominent acting company, the Lord Chamberlain's Men, when they received payment for court performances during the 1594 Christmas season.

Clearly, Shakespeare had achieved both success and reputation in London. In 1596, upon Shakespeare's application, the College of Arms granted his father the now-familiar coat of arms he had taken the first steps to obtain almost twenty years before, and in 1598, John's son – now permitted to call himself "gentleman" – took a 10 percent share in the new Globe playhouse. In 1597, he bought a substantial bourgeois house, called New Place, in Stratford – the garden remains, but Shakespeare's house, several times rebuilt, was torn down in 1759 – and over the next few years Shakespeare spent large sums buying land and making other investments in the town and its environs. Though he worked in London, his family remained in Stratford, and he seems always to have considered Stratford the home he would eventually return to. Something approaching a disinterested appreciation of Shakespeare's popular and professional status appears in Francis Meres's *Palladis Tamia* (1598), a not especially imaginative and perhaps therefore persuasive record of literary reputations. Reviewing contemporary English writers, Meres lists the titles of many of Shakespeare's plays, including one not now known, *Love's Labor's Won,* and praises his "mellifluous & hony-tongued" "sugred Sonnets," which were then circulating in manuscript (they were first collected in 1609). Meres describes Shakespeare as "one of the best" English playwrights of both comedy and tragedy. In *Remains . . . Concerning Britain* (1605), William Camden – a more authoritative source than the imitative Meres – calls Shakespeare one of the "most pregnant witts of these our times" and joins him with such writers as Chapman, Daniel, Jonson, Marston, and Spenser. During the first decades of the seventeenth century, publishers began to attribute numerous play quartos, including some non-Shakespearean ones, to Shakespeare, either by name or initials, and we may assume that they deemed Shakespeare's name and supposed authorship, true or false, commercially attractive.

For the next ten years or so, various records show

Shakespeare's dual career as playwright and man of the theater in London, and as an important local figure in Stratford. In 1608-9 his acting company – designated the "King's Men" soon after King James had succeeded Queen Elizabeth in 1603 – rented, refurbished, and opened a small interior playing space, the Blackfriars theater, in London, and Shakespeare was once again listed as a substantial sharer in the group of proprietors of the playhouse. By May 11, 1612, however, he describes himself as a Stratford resident in a London lawsuit – an indication that he had withdrawn from day-to-day professional activity and returned to the town where he had always had his main financial interests. When Shakespeare bought a substantial residential building in London, the Blackfriars Gatehouse, close to the theater of the same name, on March 10, 1613, he is recorded as William Shakespeare "of Stratford upon Avon in the county of Warwick, gentleman," and he named several London residents as the building's trustees. Still, he continued to participate in theatrical activity: when the new Earl of Rutland needed an allegorical design to bear as a shield, or *impresa,* at the celebration of King James's Accession Day, March 24, 1613, the earl's accountant recorded a payment of 44 shillings to Shakespeare for the device with its motto.

For the last few years of his life, Shakespeare evidently concentrated his activities in the town of his birth. Most of the final records concern business transactions in Stratford, ending with the notation of his death on April 23, 1616, and burial in Holy Trinity Church, Stratford-upon-Avon.

THE QUESTION OF AUTHORSHIP

The history of ascribing Shakespeare's plays (the poems do not come up so often) to someone else began, as it continues, peculiarly. The earliest published claim that someone else wrote Shakespeare's plays appeared in an 1856 article by Delia Bacon in the American journal *Putnam's Monthly* – although an Englishman, Thomas Wilmot, had shared his doubts in private (even secretive) conversations with friends near the end of the eighteenth century. Bacon's was a sad personal history that ended in madness and poverty, but the year after her article, she published, with great difficulty and the bemused assistance of Nathaniel Hawthorne (then United States Consul in Liverpool, England), her *Philosophy of the Plays of Shakspere Unfolded*. This huge, ornately written, confusing farrago is almost unreadable; sometimes its intents, to say nothing of its arguments, disappear entirely beneath near-raving, ecstatic writing. Tumbled in with much supposed "philosophy" appear the claims that Francis Bacon (from whom Delia Bacon eventually claimed descent), Walter Ralegh, and several other contemporaries of Shakespeare's had written the plays. The book had little impact except as a ridiculed curiosity.

Once proposed, however, the issue gained momentum among people whose conviction was the greater in proportion to their ignorance of sixteenth- and seventeenth-century English literature, history, and society. Another American amateur, Catherine P. Ashmead Windle, made the next influential contribution to the cause when she published *Report to the British Museum* (1882), wherein she promised to open "the Cipher of Francis Bacon," though what she mostly offers, in the words of S. Schoenbaum, is "demented allegorizing." An entire new cottage industry grew from Windle's suggestion that the texts contain hidden, cryptographically discoverable ciphers – "clues" – to their authorship; and today there are not only books devoted to the putative ciphers, but also pamphlets, journals, and newsletters.

Although Baconians have led the pack of those seeking a substitute Shakespeare, in *"Shakespeare" Identified* (1920), J. Thomas Looney became the first published

"Oxfordian" when he proposed Edward de Vere, seventeenth earl of Oxford, as the secret author of Shakespeare's plays. Also for Oxford and his "authorship" there are today dedicated societies, articles, journals, and books. Less popular candidates – Queen Elizabeth and Christopher Marlowe among them – have had adherents, but the movement seems to have divided into two main contending factions, Baconian and Oxfordian. (For further details on all the candidates for "Shakespeare," see S. Schoenbaum, *Shakespeare's Lives,* 2nd ed., 1991.)

The Baconians, the Oxfordians, and supporters of other candidates have one trait in common – they are snobs. Every pro-Bacon or pro-Oxford tract sooner or later claims that the historical William Shakespeare of Stratford-upon-Avon could not have written the plays because he could not have had the training, the university education, the experience, and indeed the imagination or background their author supposedly possessed. Only a learned genius like Bacon or an aristocrat like Oxford could have written such fine plays. (As it happens, lucky male children of the middle class had access to better education than most aristocrats in Elizabethan England – and Oxford was not particularly well educated.) Shakespeare received in the Stratford grammar school a formal education that would daunt many college graduates today; and popular rival playwrights such as the very learned Ben Jonson and George Chapman, both of whom also lacked university training, achieved great artistic success, without being taken as Bacon or Oxford.

Besides snobbery, one other quality characterizes the authorship controversy: lack of evidence. A great deal of testimony from Shakespeare's time shows that Shakespeare wrote Shakespeare's plays and that his contemporaries recognized them as distinctive and distinctly superior. (Some of that contemporary evidence is collected in E. K. Chambers, *William Shakespeare: A Study of Facts and Problems,* 2 vols., 1930.) Since that testimony comes from Shakespeare's enemies and theatrical competitors as well as from his co-workers and from the Elizabethan equivalent of literary journalists, it seems unlikely that, if any of these sources had known he was a fraud, they would have failed to record that fact.

Books About Shakespeare's Theater

Useful scholarly studies of theatrical life in Shakespeare's day include: G. E. Bentley, *The Jacobean and Caroline Stage,* 7 vols. (1941-68), and the same author's *The Professions of Dramatist and Player in Shakespeare's Time, 1590-1642* (1986); E. K. Chambers, *The Elizabethan Stage,* 4 vols. (1923); R. A. Foakes, *Illustrations of the English Stage, 1580-1642* (1985); Andrew Gurr, *The Shakespearean Stage,* 3rd ed. (1992), and the same author's *Play-going in Shakespeare's London,* 2nd ed. (1996); Edwin Nungezer, *A Dictionary of Actors* (1929); Carol Chillington Rutter, ed., *Documents of the Rose Playhouse* (1984).

Books About Shakespeare's Life

The following books provide scholarly, documented accounts of Shakespeare's life: G. E. Bentley, *Shakespeare: A Biographical Handbook* (1961); E. K. Chambers, *William Shakespeare: A Study of Facts and Problems,* 2 vols. (1930); S. Schoenbaum, *William Shakespeare: A Compact Documentary Life* (1977); and *Shakespeare's Lives,* 2nd ed. (1991), by the same author. Many scholarly editions of Shakespeare's complete works print brief compilations of essential dates and events. References to Shakespeare's works up to 1700 are collected in C. M. Ingleby et al., *The Shakespeare Allusion-Book,* rev. ed., 2 vols. (1932).

The Texts of Shakespeare

As far as we know, only one manuscript conceivably in Shakespeare's own hand may (and even this is much disputed) exist: a few pages of a play called *Sir Thomas More,* which apparently was never performed. What we do have, as later readers, performers, scholars, students, are printed texts. The earliest of these survive in two forms: quartos and folios. Quartos (from the Latin for "four") are small books, printed on sheets of paper that were then folded twice, to make four leaves or eight pages. When these were bound together, the result was a squarish, eminently portable volume that sold for the relatively small sum of sixpence (translating in modern terms to about $5.00). In folios, on the other hand, the sheets are folded only once, in half, producing large, impressive volumes taller than they are wide. This was the format for important works of philosophy, science, theology, and literature (the major precedent for a folio Shakespeare was Ben Jonson's *Works,* 1616). The decision to print the works of a popular playwright in folio is an indication of how far up on the social scale the theatrical profession had come during Shakespeare's lifetime. The Shakespeare folio was an expensive book, selling for between fifteen and eighteen shillings, depending on the binding (in modern terms, from about $150 to $180). Twenty Shakespeare plays of the thirty-seven that survive first appeared in quarto, seventeen of which appeared during Shakespeare's lifetime; the rest of the plays are found only in folio.

The First Folio was published in 1623, seven years after Shakespeare's death, and was authorized by his fellow actors, the co-owners of the King's Men. This publication was certainly a mark of the company's enormous respect for Shakespeare; but it was also a way of turning the old plays, most of which were no longer current in the play-house, into ready money (the folio includes only Shake-speare's plays, not his sonnets or other nondramatic verse). Whatever the motives behind the publication of the folio, the texts it preserves constitute the basis for almost all later editions of the playwright's works. The texts, however, dif-fer from those of the earlier quartos, sometimes in minor respects but often significantly – most strikingly in the two texts of *King Lear,* but also in important ways in *Hamlet, Othello,* and *Troilus and Cressida.* (The variants are recorded in the textual notes to each play in the new Pelican series.) The differences in these texts represent, in a sense, the essence of theater: the texts of plays were ini-tially not intended for publication. They were scripts, de-signed for the actors to perform – the principal life of the play at this period was in performance. And it follows that in Shakespeare's theater the playwright typically had no say either in how his play was performed or in the disposi-tion of his text – he was an employee of the company. The authoritative figures in the theatrical enterprise were the shareholders in the company, who were for the most part the major actors. They decided what plays were to be done; they hired the playwright and often gave him an outline of the play they wanted him to write. Often, too, the play was a collaboration: the company would retain a group of writers, and parcel out the scenes among them. The resulting script was then the property of the com-pany, and the actors would revise it as they saw fit during the course of putting it on stage. The resulting text be-longed to the company. The playwright had no rights in it once he had been paid. (This system survives largely intact in the movie industry, and most of the playwrights of Shakespeare's time were as anonymous as most screenwrit-ers are today.) The script could also, of course, continue to change as the tastes of audiences and the requirements of the actors changed. Many – perhaps most – plays were re-vised when they were reintroduced after any substantial absence from the repertory, or when they were performed by a company different from the one that originally commissioned the play.

Shakespeare was an exceptional figure in this world because he was not only a shareholder and actor in his company, but also its leading playwright – he was literally his own boss. He had, moreover, little interest in the publication of his plays, and even those that appeared during his lifetime with the authorization of the company show no signs of any editorial concern on the part of the author. Theater was, for Shakespeare, a fluid and supremely responsive medium – the very opposite of the great classic canonical text that has embodied his works since 1623.

The very fluidity of the original texts, however, has meant that Shakespeare has always had to be edited. Here is an example of how problematic the editorial project inevitably is, a passage from the most famous speech in *Romeo and Juliet,* Juliet's balcony soliloquy beginning "O Romeo, Romeo, wherefore art thou Romeo?" Since the eighteenth century, the standard modern text has read,

> What's Montague? It is nor hand, nor foot,
> Nor arm, nor face, nor any other part
> Belonging to a man. O be some other name!
> What's in a name? That which we call a rose
> By any other name would smell as sweet.
> (II.2.40–44)

Editors have three early texts of this play to work from, two quarto texts and the folio. Here is how the First Quarto (1597) reads:

> Whats *Mountague?* It is nor hand nor foote,
> Nor arme, nor face, nor any other part.
> Whats in a name? That which we call a Rofe,
> By any other name would fmell as fweet:

Here is the Second Quarto (1599):

> Whats *Mountague*? it is nor hand nor foote,
> Nor arme nor face, ô be some other name
> Belonging to a man.
> Whats in a name that which we call a rose,
> By any other word would smell as sweete,

And here is the First Folio (1623):

> What's *Mountague*? it is nor hand nor foote,
> Nor arme, nor face, O be some other name
> Belonging to a man.
> What? in a names that which we call a Rose,
> By any other word would smell as sweete,

There is in fact no early text that reads as our modern text does – and this is the most famous speech in the play. Instead, we have three quite different texts, all of which are clearly some version of the same speech, but none of which seems to us a final or satisfactory version. The transcendently beautiful passage in modern editions is an editorial invention: editors have succeeded in conflating and revising the three versions into something we recognize as great poetry. Is this what Shakespeare "really" wrote? Who can say? What we can say is that Shakespeare always had performance, not a book, in mind.

Books About the Shakespeare Texts

The standard study of the printing history of the First Folio is W. W. Greg, *The Shakespeare First Folio* (1955). J. K. Walton, *The Quarto Copy for the First Folio of Shakespeare* (1971), is a useful survey of the relation of the quartos to the folio. The second edition of Charlton Hinman's *Norton Facsimile* of the First Folio (1996), with a new introduction by Peter Blayney, is indispensable. Stanley Wells, Gary Taylor, John Jowett, and William Montgomery, *William Shakespeare: A Textual Companion,* keyed to the Oxford text, gives a comprehensive survey of the editorial situation for all the plays and poems.

THE GENERAL EDITORS

Introduction

PERHAPS MORE THAN ANY other of Shakespeare's English history plays, *1 Henry IV* displays his unique redefinition of what we understand history to be. Brisk in its pacing, restless in its shifting of scenic locations and perspectives, the play in its very tempo and texture embodies the paradoxical divisiveness and single-mindedness of civil war itself. Written sometime in the years 1596-97, and entered in the Stationers' Register on February 25, 1598, *1 Henry IV* finds Shakespeare realizing the height of his techniques in the history play form. The episodic sequencing of the *Henry VI* plays, the charismatic and dominating character concerns of *Richard III*, and the poetic textures of *Richard II* come together in this play to produce a work that is engaged both with the large processes of national events and the individual development of a fit ruler.

This play occurs near the apex of Shakespeare's exploration of a popular new genre of London theater in the 1590s. In the fourth decade of Elizabeth I's reign, and in the wake of tiny England's improbable victory over the renowned Spanish Armada in 1588, there was an appetite for the multiple forms of national history, whether printed prose histories, poetic renderings of noted incidents, or the plethora of stage treatments. The events leading to the establishment of the Tudor dynasty, of which Elizabeth I was the latest and longest-ruling scion, provided Shakespeare and others with rich material for an exploration of their country's political institutions. In particular, the question of the monarchy itself was of mesmerizing importance, and the example of the notoriously successful (if short-lived) Henry V, who appears in his youth in this play as Prince Hal, was prime dramatic material for exploring the question of what constituted a model of a Christian king.

Shakespeare's contribution to the imagination of national history is one in which the power of human subjects and effects rivals that of divine providence. Uncannily enough, this play takes as its subject the erosion of the old sacred certainties and their replacement by a new kind of historical agency and process. *1 Henry IV* is the second play of what we call Shakespeare's "second tetralogy," which, perversely, attends to the earlier part of the fifteenth-century historical record with which his history plays are largely concerned, although it was written after the plays addressing the events just prior to the arrival of Henry Tudor in 1485 (*Henry VI,* parts 1-3, and *Richard III*). *1 Henry IV* follows *Richard II* in its exploration of the consequences that follow from the disruption of dynastic order and the deposition and death of God's anointed ruler by the design of the enigmatic and politically savvy Henry Bolingbroke, now Henry IV.

Hence we find, upon the play's opening, the new king in the middle of things. He may well be desirous of mounting a crusade to Jerusalem – whether to atone for his method of securing the throne or in order to, as he later advises his son in *2 Henry IV,* "busy giddy minds / With foreign quarrels" (IV.5.213-14). But he finds himself nonetheless still caught in the "furious close of civil butchery" (I.1.13). His reputed rival for the throne, Edmund Mortimer –"proclaimed / By Richard that dead is, the next of blood" (I.3.145-46) – having been sent to suppress a Welsh uprising, has instead formed an alliance by marriage with the Welsh rebel Glendower. The Northumberland nobles, the Percy clan, are also restive in their loyalty. Hotspur (Harry Percy) is refusing to turn over his prisoners, and while he claims he objected merely to the manner of the request for them, it soon becomes clear that larger issues of allegiance are at stake. However possessed of political skills, Henry IV lacks the confidence and authority of sacred majesty. The old world of providential causes and patrilineal order has given way to one where power belongs to those who can most successfully claim it, by force or other means. Beset by civil quarrel, and seemingly abandoned by a son inattentive to the responsibilities of rule, Henry IV seems ill-suited to the new political order (and disorder) his accession to the throne has unleashed. Ironically, in a play that bears his name, Henry IV is rarely in view – as rarely, perhaps, as he seems in complete control of his realm or his eldest son. It is a telling absence.

Shakespeare sustains this opening sense of order disrupted and decentered by means of a careful and incessant dislocation of scenes. The initial venue of the court, of nobles and negotiations, quickly gives way to the apparently antithetical universe of the tavern world, where it might as well be, as Hal tells Falstaff, that "hours [are] cups of sack, and minutes capons" (I.2.7). As soon as we adjust to norms of that universe, he shifts us again, back to the court and the gathering of the rebels, where Hotspur and his uncles fulminate against the abuses they feel perpetrated upon them by the "unthankful king" and "forgetful man" (I.3.136, 162) (for whom they had, in *Richard II,* helped to prepare a way to the throne). This repeated tripartite displacement from location to location continues throughout much of the play, until the inhabitants of all three worlds converge upon the battlefield, in Act V. In the process our certainties about the values we believe each world to embody are called into question.

The play opens, for instance, with an insistence on the difference between order and disorder: Henry IV is convinced not only of his own right to suppress the unrest of the peripheral Welsh and Scottish borders, and any who would defect to them (for example, "revolted Mortimer," I.3.92), but he is also convinced, regretfully so, of the virtue of the valorous Hotspur when compared to the "riot and dishonor" (I.1.85) of his own wayward Hal. Shakespeare's alteration of historical fact so that Henry Percy and Prince Hal appear of an age serves to accentuate this contrast – in reality, Hotspur was a contemporary of

Henry IV. And while the rebels might dispute Henry's claim to speak for political order – they consider themselves the true standard-bearers of royal tradition – they share the king's conviction that there is a difference between right and rebellion, and concur that the "same sword-and-buckler Prince of Wales" (I.3.230) embodies the latter. When we arrive at the tavern, it seems as if this consensus about its disorderly nature is borne out. Hal and his companions drink and wench, pun and playact, rob and revel. If both king and rebels are agreed on the subversiveness of the tavern world, the mocking improvisations of both court and rebel camp by the tavern dwellers reveal a similar contempt for what they regard as a shared self-importance. Such a perspective makes it difficult for us subsequently to regard the assumptions of king and rebels with the gravity with which they take themselves, for we recognize the force and aptness of the parodies.

The contrast of Hotspur and Falstaff seems to emblematize this difference between law and license, and Shakespeare takes care to put the dichotomy before us. Hotspur is the "theme of honor's tongue" (I.1.81), too valiant for his own good, brave to the point of recklessness, and concerned for his reputation in "chronicles in time to come" (I.3.172). He is uncomfortable when not in battle and, though wed to the engagingly feisty Lady Percy, has little time for what he considers nonmanly, meaning nonmilitary, activities. "This is no world / To play with mammets and to tilt with lips" (II.3.89-90) are his parting words to her. Hotspur has a similar contempt for his new ally Glendower. He mistakes the latter's exorbitant verbal flights for foolish superstition and disdains the Welshman's colonial status: "I think there's no man speaks better Welsh" (III.1.50). Hotspur's world is the traditional one of "History," a record of events written by the winners, of the doings of great men enacting God's design, with little recognition of what goes on behind the scenes of battle. He is as ill at ease with political negotiation as he is with domestic life.

This is not, however, Shakespeare's historical world. The very fact of his inclusion of the tavern universe in his "history" play, and his celebration of its presiding genius, most signals his departure from the world of providential chronicle record. Falstaff, unlike Hotspur, has little patience with the abstractions of honor or chivalry: "Can honor set to a leg? No" (V.1.131). His allegiance is not to fine ideas and abstractions, however noble or high-minded, but to the body: its wants, its pleasures, its pains. Unlike Hotspur, he loves wine, women, and song, he enjoys verbal play, and, despite his knightly rank (remember, he is *Sir* John Falstaff), he is most at home in the margins of society, the Eastcheap tavern (which of course is also the heart of urban London, much as the court is its head). Old, fat, always ready for a cup of sack or a juicy capon or a wench on his knee, Falstaff is most appealing when defending his girth and saving his skin, lying and playacting. He is unafraid to mock Henry IV and his values or to tease Hal about the provenance of his royalty: "Should I turn upon the true prince?" (II.4.258) he asks, ironically, displaying a rather wry regard for the putative sanctity of the claim to the throne by "the heir apparent" (II.4.258). We delight in his lies, his bombast, and his practical priorities, and most of all in his dedication to *life*. Like Chaucer's Wife of Bath, he is a character who takes on a life beyond the play, and almost seems to exist independent of the circumstances of his creation; so popular was he that even in Shakespeare's time Queen Elizabeth reputedly asked to see him in a play of his own, and in love.

Falstaff is least appealing when he must leave the tavern for the battlefield. When he impresses "food for powder" (IV.2.64–65) rather than fit soldiers in order to increase his own purse, and produces a bottle of sack when Hal calls for a pistol on the battlefield, we wince for his bad judgment and bad timing. He has, as he well knows, all of the charisma and lurid appeal of "that reverend Vice" (II.4.438), that dynamic figure in a morality play whom the hero must reluctantly renounce in order to follow his good angel.

Shakespeare's invocation of the morality play structure is not casual here; Prince Hal does stand as a kind of Everyman figure in relation to these two models, foils to each other as well as to the prince, and part of the play's suspense revolves around the prospect of his renunciation of one path in favor of another. The stage picture in Act V, scene 4, when Hal stands poised between the two bodies of the brave soldier and the fat knight, underscores this thematic structure. But as ever with Shakespeare, no choice, and no dramatic structure, is ever that simple. Hal may seem to eschew the foolery of Falstaff in favor of military glory, challenging Hotspur to single combat and distinguishing himself in the arena of war. But it is Hotspur who lies dead at the end of this play, and Falstaff, ever vital, bounds up, to lie another day, Christ-like, as well as Vice-like, in his resurrection. In this very resolution Shakespeare calls into question the simple notions of Hal's choices, as well as our reliance on the balanced symmetries and clear antitheses with which we structure our ethical and historical tales. Is Falstaff's resurrection a case of the bad angel firing the good one out, or its opposite? Or are such terms even appropriate here?

Indeed, as with the dislocating structural rhythms of the play, in which the values of one world supplant those of another, and are in turn themselves overturned, the opposition of Hal's foils is never an easy one. Hotspur, for all his claim to traditional notions of masculine prowess, is nonetheless, in his blindly passionate commitment to his ideals, subject to accusations of "this woman's mood" (I.3.237) when he yields to his temper and neglects the advice of Worcester and his father, Northumberland. Though he disdains as foolishly superstitious Glendower's claims to supernatural forces, he himself, amazingly enough, thinks to redirect the course of the River Trent in order to secure what he considers his just share of the British isle. Most damning of all, he lacks political savvy:

a fault that leads to his death, as his co-partners in rebellion manipulate his lust for honor in order to refuse Henry's offer of a truce. The very qualities that make him a brave warrior render him vulnerable to the machinations of true politicians. Hotspur is ultimately the tragic figure of the play, caught by his own flaws in a machinery larger than his own power to direct it.

Conversely, Falstaff, for all his impropriety on the field of war, is far more politically astute than Hotspur: able to bluff, to bide his time, and to perceive the truth behind appearances, the realpolitik through the rhetoric ("rebellion lay in his way, and he found it," V.1.28, he comments upon Worcester's disavowal of his part in civil war). Ultimately, he is a survivor. As they reverse each other on the score of honor, so do they also on the score of political acumen – which perhaps suggests why it is Falstaff, and not Hotspur, who accompanies Hal off the battlefield. Even more tellingly, Falstaff's historical identity underscores his emotional power in the play. If Hotspur, in record, was twice Hal's age, Falstaff was once Sir John Oldcastle ("my old lad of the castle," I.2.41-42, as Hal calls him), a proto-Protestant martyr, killed at the order of the king for his religious faith. While this identity, like Hotspur's true age, is all but absent from the play (Shakespeare was forced to change the name at the objection of Oldcastle's descendants), the force of Hal's affiliation with Falstaff owes something to this former life and its great sentimental importance to Elizabethan England.

The way in which Falstaff and Hotspur alike defy type is instructive, for it is a habit of this play to subvert simple oppositions as well as easy symmetries. Perhaps most obvious is that between "order" and "rebellion." The very attempt of both Henry IV and his opponents to speak for the former raises the question of the priority of any one claim. From Henry's point of view, the rebels (as Blunt puts it) "out of limit and true rule / . . . stand against anointed majesty" (IV.3.39-40); for Hotspur and his party, the king – or Bolingbroke, as they prefer to call him – holds a title "Too indirect for long continuance" (IV.3.105). How are we to arbitrate between these claims to the throne? Who owns the language of right and order? Or is it just a language, to be spoken more or less convincingly by any speaker who chooses?

Perhaps even more disorienting to simple oppositions between law and misrule is the example of the tavern. For life in the tavern is not simply fun and games, heedless of the serious matters of political life, as both Henry IV and Hotspur believe. Or, rather, like much fun and many games, they perform an earnest function. When Hal teases the drawer Francis with visions of defecting on his apprenticeship, he may seem to speak for license and law-breaking, but he is also enacting a complicated, and rather disturbing, show of his own power over the servant, who is unable to ignore the prince's nonsensical questions despite the competing call of duty to his employment. While Hal claims to be able to "drink with any tinker in his own language" (II.4.18), he scorns the tongue-tied fumbling of Francis, despite being its primary cause: "That ever this fellow should have fewer words than a parrot, and yet the son of a woman!" (II.4.94–95). He is more cruel than comradely here. Similarly, though Hal participates in the Gad's Hill robbery by robbing the robbers, his participation results in the restoration of the purses to their rightful owners. So too, when he proposes to mock Hotspur or his father in theatrical play, he displays a keen awareness of the proper hierarchies of political life: "I do, I will," he assures "plump Jack" (II.4.465, 464) with respect to his banishment – a promise on which he will indeed one day make good. Furthermore, in playfully mocking the scene of his confrontation with his father, he also rehearses for it, and is all the more prepared for the real event when it arrives.

So if the competing aspirants to order are themselves subject to charges of rebellion, so the denizens of the tavern are not as unruly as they might seem. In fact, our experience of the play reveals an uncanny similarity among all three worlds when it comes to a mixture of law and license. The tavern denizens may be stealing "purses," but the rebels are, from the perspective of the king, a pack of robbing "Percies," a word that, in the pronunciation of Elizabeth English, links them uncomfortably closely with the tavern activity. And Henry IV, we must remember, stands accused of stealing crowns (a denomination of Elizabethan coin as well as a prop of rule). No one faction in this world has a monopoly on the language of rule, or of rule-breaking.

It is appropriate that a pun secures the similarities of these worlds that would claim such difference from each other. For what a pun does is change the value of a heretofore stable and singular meaning. In fact, it is no coincidence that it is in punning, and in "quips" and "quiddities" (I.2.45) that Prince Hal excels, and this talent perhaps suggests why his particular model of political action is marked to succeed in a world of shifting values. Rhetorical fluency is his forte, whether it be tinkers' drinking tongues, fat and skinny insult contests with Falstaff, or the courtly rhetoric of his father. Indeed, it is the ability to move among those worlds that marks Hal as the most politically gifted character of the play. He resembles nothing so much as an actor, able to take on the guise most likely to serve his purpose: the barroom crony, the prince of good fellows, the penitent son, or the chivalrous challenger. Like us, the audience, Prince Hal possesses the ability to move between worlds, negotiating the protocols of each with equal dexterity.

In creating the character of Prince Hal, Shakespeare had a powerful historical myth with which to work. The prince of chronicle record (Shakespeare relied chiefly on Holinshed's *Chronicles*) was already the hero of other history plays at this time, and was notorious both for his wayward youth and his extraordinary success as a ruler. Legend had it that as a prince he was jailed for striking the chief justice, whereas as a king he went on to govern, however briefly, a peaceful England and to lead a victorious campaign against the French, winning against all odds the battle at Agincourt. It was the stuff of myth – a story of a prodigal son, of a miraculous conversion, and of a reformation of biblical contours. Shakespeare makes his portrait of the prince all the more powerful in that he portrays Hal as in control of this legend from the start, as if he knew beforehand the historical place he would come to occupy. Indeed, what his portrait communicates is that this incipient mirror of all Christian kings was, even in his infancy, a master of rhetorical appearances. In short, he is a consummately theatrical ruler. If Hal has, in Henry IV and Falstaff, two father figures, it may be Falstaff, the actor and liar, to whom he is most indebted in this world where power belongs to those best able to improvise in response to constantly changing circumstances. The moment in battle at Shrewsbury, when several warriors "march" in the "king's coats" (V.3.25) in order to serve as decoys for enemy attack, epitomizes the way in which royalty has come to rely less on a sacred and divine presence than a strategic and theatrical deployment of royal representations. Henry IV may think his power is best protected in its rarity and remoteness; his son, however, plunges into the fray, only in order to rise, phoenixlike, from it.

Prince Hal is a master of the imagery of kingship, and we see this quality in Hal from our first moment alone with him, at the end of Act I, scene 2. On the heels of his agreement to participate in the robbery, Hal addresses us in soliloquy, that actorly index of intimacy and sincerity. Here he unveils to his auditors that his sojourn in the tavern world is not, in truth, a vacation from his future duty and identity (he is well aware he will "imitate the sun," I.2.190), but a crucial preparation for the myth of his prodigal conversion: "like bright metal on a sullen ground, / My reformation, glitt'ring o'er my fault, / Shall show more goodly and attract more eyes / Than that which hath no foil to set it off" (I.2.205-8). In effect, he tells us, he is using his tavern companions less to acquaint himself with the ways of his future subjects than to prepare the way for his surprise attack on the role of future king. His story is not that of Everyman caught between a good and bad angel at all, but rather that of the prodigal son, all the more welcome home for his errant departure from duty (and for whom the fatted calf is killed). Hal is throughout portrayed as in complete control of his own mythology, and never mistaken about his own royal identity, as "the sun, / Who doth permit the base contagious clouds / To smother up his beauty from the world" (I.2.190-92). When his father rebukes him for overfamiliarity with the baser sort, for having "lost thy princely privilege / With vile participation" III.2.86-87), and urging his own royal metaphor of a "comet," "Ne'er seen but wondered at" (III.2.57), Hal seizes the opportunity to begin his astounding reformation with a stirring promise of penitence and reparation. (What Henry seems to have forgotten here is his own popular approach to the throne, his once having doffed his cap, in the contemptuous phrase of Richard II, "to an oyster wench" [*Richard II,* I.4].) Hal, however, never having taken the sign of royalty for literal truth, can easily move among the necessary symbols as the occasion requires.

What the figure of Prince Hal conveys is that to be king in this world is to know how to manipulate signs and symbols and stories, to be master of all, but believe in none, or only to the outwardly convincing extent that is required to compel the belief of others. He is a complex figure, and our reponses to him are too. Take the moment of his soliloquy: on the one hand, Hal graces us with his confidence; on the other, it is a confidence that he is in fact using the very companions who have taken him into theirs, who have in good faith promised him that when he is "King of England [he] shall command all the good lads in Eastcheap" (II.4.13-14). Despite the fact that dramatic soliloquy usually encourages a kind of kinship with the figure who speaks to us, such a proximity to Prince Hal is problematic, partly, indeed, because of his rhetorical mastery: one is never quite sure what he means or how to weigh certain words and meanings. What, in fact, can it mean of such a thoroughly theatrical self when he promises his father, "I shall hereafter, my thrice-gracious lord, / Be more myself" (III.2.92-93)? Who is he? While he seems to have a certain affection for Falstaff, to feel chastened by his father, and to be stung by the example of Hotspur, the key word is "seems." (In this aspect he resembles Hamlet, another young prince in a world of shifting appearances.) The moment of the joint eulogies over the bodies of Hotspur and Falstaff is paradigmatic, full of doublespeak and hidden ironies, of puns that cavil with our sense of poignancy even as they conjure it.

The political animal that emerges in Prince Hal's portrait is not one to whom we feel especially close; his sentimental appeal is always a guarded one (unlike Falstaff's, whom it is possible to out and out adore as well as be embarrassed by). The prince's ability to stage-manage his own reformation seems Machiavellian, and hence inspires suspicion: as a figure of a man, or a friend, or even a son, he is not trustworthy. Despite the demystifying gesture of his soliloquy, he remains a cipher. As a prospective ruler, however, Hal does inspire confidence, and even admiration. For it is in his command of language and appearance that he is best suited to thrive in this new world, and perhaps allow others to thrive with him. When he allows Falstaff to claim credit for delivering Hotspur's death blow, he promises to make his dissolute friend appear in a glorious light, and hence, potentially, himself as well; and given that no one will believe Falstaff capable of such a thing, the prince reaps a double profit, in acquiring a reputation for selflessness. It is a complex and not altogether savory act. Nor is its meaning entirely clear. But proximity, or legibility, may not be what we want most of our rulers.

CLAIRE MCEACHERN
University of California at Los Angeles

Note on the Text

THE PRESENT TEXT FOLLOWS, with only a few emendations, that of the First Quarto (1598), which is believed to have been printed from the author's draft. In the folio text of 1623, printed from the Fifth Quarto (1613), the play was first divided into acts and scenes. The act-scene division supplied in the present text is that of the folio except that V.2 of the folio is divided into two scenes. Below are listed all substantive departures from the quarto text, with the adopted reading in italics followed by the quarto reading in roman. The designation Q0 represent a quarto of which only four leaves survive. It was probably published in 1598 and served as copy for Q1.

I.1   30 *Therefor* (ed.) Therefore   62 *a dear* (Q5) deere   69 *blood* (Q5) bloud.

I.2   33 *moon . . . proof now:* (Rowe) moone, . . . proofe. Now   79 *similes* (Q5) smiles   111 *Sugar? Jack,* (Capell) Sugar Iacke?   122 *Gad's Hill* (Wilson) Gadshill   153 *thou* (Pope) the   157 *Bardolph* (Theobald) Haruey; *Peto* (Dering) Rossill

I.3   96 *tongue* (Hanmer) tongue: 139 *struck* (Malone) strooke   201 *HOTSPUR* (Q5) Omitted (Q1)   254 *for I* (F) I   262 *granted . . . lord,* (Thirlby) granted . . . Lord.   290 *course.* (Johnson) course

II.1   34 *FIRST CARRIER* (Hanmer) Car.   74 *foot landrakers* (Hanmer) foot-lande rakers

II.2   16 *two-and-twenty* (F) xxii   20 (and throughout the play) *Bardolph* (F) Bardoll (or Bardol)   41 *Go hang* (Q3) Hang   50 *BARDOLPH What* (Johnson) Bardoll, what   51 *GADSHILL* (Johnson) Bar.   82 *Ah* (Rowe) a   106 *fat rogue* (Q0) rogue

II.3   4 *In respect* (Q6) in the respect   46 *thee* (Q2) the   68 *A roan* (Q3) Roane

II.4   32 *precedent* (F: President) present   114 *(pitiful-hearted Titan!)* (Warburton) pittiful harted titan   166 *PRINCE* (Dering) Gads.   167, 169, 173 *GADSHILL* (F) Ross.   235 *eel-skin* (Hanmer) elsskin   291 *Tell* (F) Faith tell   328 *Owen* (Dering) O   380 *tristful* (Dering) trustfull   438 *reverend* (F) reverent   458 *lean* (Q2) lane   476 *mad* (F3) made   511 *PETO* (F) Omitted (Q1)   523 *PRINCE* (F) Omitted (Q1)

III.1   100 *cantle* (F) scantle   116 *I will* (Pope) I'le   128 *meter* (F) miter
131 *on* (Q3) an   262 *hot* (F) Hot.

III.2   110 *capital* (Q2) capitall.

III.3   35 *that's* (Q3) that   37–38 *Gad's Hill* (Wilson) Gadshill   57 *tithe*
(Theobald) tight   74 *four-and-twenty* (F) xxiiii.   118 *no thing* (Q3)
nothing   172 *guests* (Q2) ghesse   175 *court.* (Keightley) court   189
two-and-twenty (F) xxii.   200 *o'clock* (Q2) of clocke

IV.1   20 *lord* (Capell) mind   55 *Is* (F) tis   108 *dropped* (Q2) drop   116
altar (Q4) altars   126 *cannot* (Q5) can   127 *yet* (Q5) it

IV.2   3 *Sutton Co'fil'* (Cambridge eds) Sutton cophill

IV.3   21 *horse* (Q5) horses   28 *ours* (Q6) our   72 *heirs as pages,* (Singer)
heires, as Pages   82 *country's* (Q5) Countrey

V.1   25 *I do* (F) I   131 *then?* (Q2) then   137 *will it* (Q2) wil

V.2   3 *undone* (Q5) vnder one   10 *ne'er* (F) neuer   70 *Upon* (Pope) On

V.3   22 *A* (Capell) Ah   39 *stand'st* (Q2) stands   51 *get'st* (Q2) gets

V.4   33 *So* (F) and   67 *Nor* (F) Now   91 *thee* (Q7) the   156 *ours* (Q2)
our   157 *let's* (Q4) let us

V.5   36 *bend you* (Q4) bend, you

The First Part of
King Henry the Fourth

[NAMES OF THE ACTORS

The court:
KING HENRY THE FOURTH *(formerly Henry Bolingbroke)*
HENRY, PRINCE OF WALES ⎱ *the king's sons*
PRINCE JOHN OF LANCASTER ⎰
EARL OF WESTMORELAND
SIR WALTER BLUNT

The rebel camp:
THOMAS PERCY, *Earl of Worcester*
HENRY PERCY, *Earl of Northumberland*
HENRY PERCY ("HOTSPUR"), *his son*
EDMUND MORTIMER, *Earl of March*
RICHARD SCROOP, *Archbishop of York*
ARCHIBALD, *Earl of Douglas*
OWEN GLENDOWER
SIR RICHARD VERNON
SIR MICHAEL, *a friend of the Archbishop of York*
LADY PERCY, *Hotspur's wife and Mortimer's sister*
LADY MORTIMER, *Glendower's daughter*

The tavern:
SIR JOHN FALSTAFF
POINS
GADSHILL
PETO
BARDOLPH
VINTNER *of an Eastcheap Tavern*
FRANCIS, *a waiter*
MISTRESS QUICKLY, *hostess of an Eastcheap tavern*

Others:
CHAMBERLAIN *of an inn at Rochester*
OSTLER
MUGS AND ANOTHER CARRIER
TRAVELERS *on the road from Rochester to London*
SHERIFF
HOTSPUR'S SERVANT
MESSENGER FROM NORTHUMBERLAND
TWO MESSENGERS *(soldiers in Hotspur's army)*

SCENE: *England and Wales*]
*

The First Part of
King Henry the Fourth

∾ I.1 *Enter the King, Lord John of Lancaster, Earl of Westmoreland, [Sir Walter Blunt,] with others.*

KING
So shaken as we are, so wan with care,
Find we a time for frighted peace to pant   2
And breathe short-winded accents of new broils   3
To be commenced in stronds afar remote.   4
No more the thirsty entrance of this soil   5
Shall daub her lips with her own children's blood:
No more shall trenching war channel her fields,   7
Nor bruise her flowerets with the armèd hoofs
Of hostile paces. Those opposèd eyes
Which, like the meteors of a troubled heaven,   10
All of one nature, of one substance bred,
Did lately meet in the intestine shock   12
And furious close of civil butchery,   13
Shall now in mutual well-beseeming ranks   14
March all one way and be no more opposed
Against acquaintance, kindred, and allies.
The edge of war, like an ill-sheathèd knife,
No more shall cut his master. Therefore, friends,   18
As far as to the sepulcher of Christ —   19

I.1 London, the court of Henry IV **2** *Find we* let us find **3** *accents* words; *broils* battles **4** *stronds afar remote* distant shores (strands) **5** *entrance* openings, chasms **7** *trenching* plowing **12** *intestine* internal **13** *close* hand-to-hand combat **14** *mutual ... ranks* unified, orderly army formations **18** *his* its **19** *sepulcher* tomb (i.e., Jerusalem)

20 Whose soldier now, under whose blessed cross
21 We are impressèd and engaged to fight –
22 Forthwith a power of English shall we levy,
    Whose arms were molded in their mother's womb
24 To chase these pagans in those holy fields
    Over whose acres walked those blessed feet
    Which fourteen hundred years ago were nailed
27 For our advantage on the bitter cross.
    But this our purpose now is twelve month old,
29 And bootless 'tis to tell you we will go.
30 Therefor we meet not now. Then let me hear
    Of you, my gentle cousin Westmoreland,
    What yesternight our council did decree
33 In forwarding this dear expedience.

WESTMORELAND

34 My liege, this haste was hot in question
35 And many limits of the charge set down
36 But yesternight; when all athwart there came
37 A post from Wales, loaden with heavy news,
    Whose worst was that the noble Mortimer,
    Leading the men of Herefordshire to fight
40 Against the irregular and wild Glendower,
    Was by the rude hands of that Welshman taken,
42 A thousand of his people butcherèd;
    Upon whose dead corpse there was such misuse,
44 Such beastly shameless transformation,
    By those Welshwomen done as may not be
    Without much shame retold or spoken of.

---

21 *impressèd* conscripted   22 *power* force, army; *levy* raise   24 *pagans* i.e., non-Christians   27 *advantage* salvation   29 *bootless* useless   30 *Therefore . . . not* i.e., that is not why we meet   33 *dear expedience* crucial (and perhaps expensive) undertaking   34 *liege* lord; *hot in question* fiercely debated   35 *limits of the charge* items of military duties   36 *all athwart* in cross purpose   37 *post* news, a messenger; *loaden with* carrying; *heavy* sad   40 *irregular* unruly, unpredictable   42 *his* i.e., Mortimer's   44 *transformation* mutilation (Welshwomen reputedly castrated enemy bodies in battle and placed the severed genitals in the mouth of the corpse)

KING

It seems then that the tidings of this broil 47
Brake off our business for the Holy Land. 48

WESTMORELAND

This, matched with other, did, my gracious lord; 49
For more uneven and unwelcome news 50
Came from the north, and thus it did import:
On Holy-Rood Day the gallant Hotspur there, 52
Young Harry Percy, and brave Archibald,
That ever-valiant and approvèd Scot, 54
At Holmedon met, 55
Where they did spend a sad and bloody hour;
As by discharge of their artillery 57
And shape of likelihood the news was told;
For he that brought them, in the very heat 59
And pride of their contention did take horse, 60
Uncertain of the issue any way. 61

KING

Here is a dear, a true-industrious friend,
Sir Walter Blunt, new lighted from his horse, 63
Stained with the variation of each soil 64
Betwixt that Holmedon and this seat of ours, 65
And he hath brought us smooth and welcome news. 66
The Earl of Douglas is discomfited; 67
Ten thousand bold Scots, two-and-twenty knights,
Balked in their own blood did Sir Walter see 69
On Holmedon's plains. Of prisoners, Hotspur took 70
Mordake Earl of Fife and eldest son
To beaten Douglas, and the Earl of Athol,

---

47 *tidings* news   48 *Brake off* interrupt, call off   49 *other* i.e., other news
50 *uneven* disturbing   52 *Holy-Rood Day* September 14 (the Roman
Catholic feast of the exaltation of the Cross)   54 *approvèd* of proven bravery
55 *Holmedon* Humbleton, in Northumberland (in the north of England)
57–58 *As . . . likelihood* judging from the sounds of their weapons and the
probable outcome   59 *them* i.e., news   59–60 *heat . . . pride* midst and
height   61 *issue* outcome   63 *new lighted* just dismounted   64 *variation*
different kinds   65 *this seat* i.e., London   66 *smooth* pleasant   67 *discomfited* defeated   69 *Balked* heaped up   70 *Of* for

Of Murray, Angus, and Menteith.
74 And is not this an honorable spoil?
A gallant prize? Ha, cousin, is it not?

WESTMORELAND
In faith,
It is a conquest for a prince to boast of.

KING
Yea, there thou mak'st me sad, and mak'st me sin
In envy that my Lord Northumberland
80 Should be the father to so blessed a son –
A son who is the theme of honor's tongue,
Amongst a grove the very straightest plant;
83 Who is sweet fortune's minion and her pride;
Whilst I, by looking on the praise of him,
See riot and dishonor stain the brow
Of my young Harry. O, that it could be proved
That some night-tripping fairy had exchanged
In cradle clothes our children where they lay,
89 And called mine Percy, his Plantagenet!
90 Then would I have his Harry, and he mine.
But let him from my thoughts. What think you, coz,
Of this young Percy's pride? The prisoners
93 Which he in this adventure hath surprised
To his own use he keeps, and sends me word
I shall have none but Mordake Earl of Fife.

WESTMORELAND
This is his uncle's teaching, this is Worcester,
97 Malevolent to you in all aspects,
98 Which makes him prune himself and bristle up
The crest of youth against your dignity.

KING
100 But I have sent for him to answer this;
And for this cause awhile we must neglect

---

74 *spoil* booty, winnings 83 *minion* favorite 89 *Plantagenet* family name
of royalty since Henry II 93 *surprised* captured 97 *Malevolent* ill-willed
98 *him* i.e., Hotspur; *prune* preen (like a predatory bird, with a feathered
crest)

Our holy purpose to Jerusalem.
Cousin, on Wednesday next our council we
Will hold at Windsor. So inform the lords;
But come yourself with speed to us again;
For more is to be said and to be done
Than out of anger can be utterèd.

WESTMORELAND
I will, my liege.   *Exeunt.*

*

∾ **I.2** *Enter Prince of Wales and Sir John Falstaff.*

FALSTAFF   Now, Hal, what time of day is it, lad?

PRINCE   Thou art so fat-witted with drinking of old sack,   2
and unbuttoning thee after supper, and sleeping upon
benches after noon, that thou hast forgotten to demand   4
that truly which thou wouldest truly know. What a
devil hast thou to do with the time of the day? Unless
hours were cups of sack, and minutes capons, and   7
clocks the tongues of bawds, and dials the signs of leap-   8
ing houses, and the blessed sun himself a fair hot
wench in flame-colored taffeta, I see no reason why   10
thou shouldst be so superfluous to demand the time of   11
the day.

FALSTAFF   Indeed you come near me now, Hal; for we   13
that take purses go by the moon and the seven stars,   14
and not by Phoebus, he, that wand'ring knight so fair.   15
And I prithee, sweet wag, when thou art a king, as,   16

I.2 London, a room of the prince's   **2** *fat-witted* thickheaded; *sack* Spanish
white wine   **4** *benches* privy seats   **4–5** *to demand . . . know* how to ask what
you really want to know   **7** *capons* poultry (gelded male birds)   **8** *bawds*
prostitutes   **8–9** *leaping houses* brothels   **10** *taffeta* a stiff, shiny material fa-
vored by prostitutes   **11** *superfluous* out of your way   **13** *you come near me*
you're on to me, you have me there   **14** *take purses* rob (with a pun on thieving "Percies"?); *go by* travel by the light of, tell time by; *seven stars* the Pleiades
15 *Phoebus* the sun god (compared to a traveling knight)   **16** *wag* fool,
scamp

17 God save thy grace – majesty I should say, for grace
thou wilt have none –

PRINCE What, none?

20 FALSTAFF No, by my troth; not so much as will serve to
21 be prologue to an egg and butter.

22 PRINCE Well, how then? Come, roundly, roundly.

23 FALSTAFF Marry, then, sweet wag, when thou art king,
24 let not us that are squires of the night's body be called
25 thieves of the day's beauty. Let us be Diana's foresters,
gentlemen of the shade, minions of the moon; and let
men say we be men of good government, being gov-
28 erned as the sea is, by our noble and chaste mistress the
29 moon, under whose countenance we steal.

30 PRINCE Thou sayest well, and it holds well too; for the
31 fortune of us that are the moon's men doth ebb and
flow like the sea, being governed, as the sea is, by the
33 moon. As, for proof now: a purse of gold most res-
34 olutely snatched on Monday night and most dissolutely spent on Tuesday morning; got with swearing
36 "Lay by," and spent with crying "Bring in"; now in as
37 low an ebb as the foot of the ladder, and by-and-by in
38 as high a flow as the ridge of the gallows.

FALSTAFF By the Lord, thou say'st true, lad – and is not
40 my hostess of the tavern a most sweet wench?

41 PRINCE As the honey of Hybla, my old lad of the

---

17 *grace* (term for royalty, spiritual grace, and prayer before meals)   20 *troth*
truth   21 *prologue* preface; *egg and butter* i.e., a snack   22 *roundly* out with
it   23 *Marry* indeed (originally an oath on the name of the Virgin Mary)
24–25 *squires . . . beauty* servants of the night be accused of stealing daylight by
sleeping during it   25 *Diana* goddess of the moon, the hunt (and of chastity?)
28 *sea* i.e., tides, governed by the moon   29 *countenance* (1) face, (2) approval;
steal (1) move stealthily, (2) rob   30 *holds well* is a good comparison   31 *fortune* lot, fate   33 *for proof* to demonstrate   33–34 *resolutely* firmly   34–35
dissolutely wastefully   36 *Lay by* hands up; *Bring in* bring me (spoken to a
tavern waiter)   37 *ladder* gallows ladder   38 *ridge* ridgepole, crossbar (from
which the noose is hung)   41 *Hybla* a town in Sicily famous for its honey
41–42 *old lad of the castle* (a play on Falstaff's original historical name [Oldcas-
tle], which was reputedly changed due to the objections of his descendants)

castle – and is not a buff jerkin a most sweet robe of   42
durance?   43

FALSTAFF   How now, how now, mad wag? What, in thy
quips and thy quiddities? What a plague have I to do   45
with a buff jerkin?

PRINCE   Why, what a pox have I to do with my hostess of   47
the tavern?

FALSTAFF   Well, thou hast called her to a reckoning many   49
a time and oft.   50

PRINCE   Did I ever call for thee to pay thy part?

FALSTAFF   No; I'll give thee thy due, thou hast paid all
there.

PRINCE   Yea, and elsewhere, so far as my coin would
stretch; and where it would not, I have used my credit.

FALSTAFF   Yea, and so used it that, were it not here apparent that thou art heir apparent – But I prithee, sweet   57
wag, shall there be gallows standing in England when
thou art king? and resolution thus fubbed as it is with   59
the rusty curb of old father antic the law? Do not thou,   60
when thou art king, hang a thief.

PRINCE   No; thou shalt.

FALSTAFF   Shall I? O rare! By the Lord, I'll be a brave
judge.

PRINCE   Thou judgest false already. I mean, thou shalt
have the hanging of the thieves and so become a rare
hangman.

FALSTAFF   Well, Hal, well; and in some sort it jumps   68
with my humor as well as waiting in the court, I can tell   69
you.   70

---

42 *buff jerkin* leather jacket worn by law officers   43 *durance* long-wearing,
imprisoning   45 *quips* clever remarks; *quiddities* quibbles, finicky points
47 *pox* venereal disease   49 *called . . . reckoning* (1) settled the bill, (2)
arranged a sexual encounter   57 *heir apparent* next in line to the throne;
prithee pray thee (please)   59 *resolution thus fubbed* brave exploits (of crimi-
nals) thwarted, frustrated   60 *curb* harsh bit (as for a horse); *antic* buffoon
68–69 *jumps with* suits   69 *humor* nature; *waiting in the court* being a
courtier

71 PRINCE   For obtaining of suits?

FALSTAFF   Yea, for obtaining of suits, whereof the hang-
73   man hath no lean wardrobe. 'Sblood, I am as melan-
74   choly as a gib-cat or a lugged bear.

PRINCE   Or an old lion, or a lover's lute.

76 FALSTAFF   Yea, or the drone of a Lincolnshire bagpipe.

77 PRINCE   What sayest thou to a hare, or the melancholy of
78   Moorditch?

FALSTAFF   Thou hast the most unsavory similes, and art
80   indeed the most comparative, rascaliest, sweet young
   prince. But, Hal, I prithee trouble me no more with
82   vanity. I would to God thou and I knew where a commodity of good names were to be bought. An old lord
84   of the council rated me the other day in the street about
   you, sir, but I marked him not; and yet he talked very
   wisely, but I regarded him not; and yet he talked wisely,
   and in the street too.

88 PRINCE   Thou didst well, for wisdom cries out in the
   streets, and no man regards it.

90 FALSTAFF   O, thou hast damnable iteration, and art indeed able to corrupt a saint. Thou hast done much
   harm upon me, Hal – God forgive thee for it! Before I
   knew thee, Hal, I knew nothing; and now am I, if a
   man should speak truly, little better than one of the
95   wicked. I must give over this life, and I will give it over!
96   By the Lord, an I do not, I am a villain! I'll be damned
   for never a king's son in Christendom.

PRINCE   Where shall we take a purse tomorrow, Jack?

---

71 *obtaining of suits* (1) acquiring the clothes of the executed, (2) achieving
answers to petitions to the king   73 *wardrobe* (the hangman was entitled to
the clothes of those hanged by him); *'Sblood* by God's (i.e., Christ's) blood
(an oath)   74 *gib-cat* tomcat (hence randy); *lugged* chained and baited by
dogs   76 *drone* keening bass sound   77 *hare* proverbially melancholy   78
Moorditch an open sewer draining Moorfields, outside London walls   80
comparative given to bad comparisons   82 *vanity* worldly concerns   82–83
commodity supply, quantity   84 *rated* berated, scolded   88–89 *wisdom . . .
it* Proverbs 1:20–24   90 *iteration* repetition of Scripture   95 *over* up   96
an if; *villain* (1) evil person, (2) peasant (villein)

FALSTAFF Zounds, where thou wilt, lad! I'll make one. 99
An I do not, call me villain and baffle me. 100

PRINCE I see a good amendment of life in thee – from
praying to purse-taking.

FALSTAFF Why, Hal, 'tis my vocation, Hal. 'Tis no sin
for a man to labor in his vocation. 104
    Enter Poins.
Poins! Now shall we know if Gadshill have set a match. 105
O, if men were to be saved by merit, what hole in hell 106
were hot enough for him? This is the most omnipotent 107
villain that ever cried "stand!" to a true man. 108

PRINCE Good morrow, Ned. 109

POINS Good morrow, sweet Hal. What says Monsieur *110*
Remorse? What says Sir John Sack and Sugar? Jack, 111
how agrees the devil and thee about thy soul, that thou
soldest him on Good Friday last for a cup of Madeira 113
and a cold capon's leg?

PRINCE Sir John stands to his word, the devil shall have 115
his bargain; for he was never yet a breaker of proverbs.
He will give the devil his due.

POINS Then art thou damned for keeping thy word with
the devil.

PRINCE Else he had been damned for cozening the devil. 120

POINS But, my lads, my lads, tomorrow morning, by
four o'clock early, at Gad's Hill! There are pilgrims 122
going to Canterbury with rich offerings, and traders 123
riding to London with fat purses. I have vizards for you 124
all; you have horses for yourselves. Gadshill lies tonight 125

---

99 *Zounds* by God's (i.e., Christ's) wounds (an oath); *make one* be there, be
of the party **100** *baffle me* disgrace in public **104** *vocation* (religious) calling **105** *Gadshill* (1) name of highway robber, (2) place on road from London to Canterbury (Gad's Hill, l. 122); *set a match* made a plan for a robbery
106 *saved by merit* earn salvation, as opposed to having it freely granted by
God **107** *omnipotent* thorough, complete **108** *stand!* hands up! **109**
morrow morning **111** *Remorse* regret, penitence **113** *Madeira* sweet Spanish wine **115** *to* by **120** *cozening* tricking, cheating **122** *pilgrims* people
traveling to a sacred place (here, the tomb of Thomas à Becket) **123** *traders*
merchants **124** *vizards* masks, visors **125** *lies* rests, stops

126   in Rochester. I have bespoke supper tomorrow night in
127   Eastcheap. We may do it as secure as sleep. If you will
        go, I will stuff your purses full of crowns; if you will
129   not, tarry at home and be hanged!

130 FALSTAFF   Hear ye, Yedward: if I tarry at home and go
        not, I'll hang you for going.

132 POINS   You will, chops?

133 FALSTAFF   Hal, wilt thou make one?

       PRINCE   Who, I rob? I a thief? Not I, by my faith.

       FALSTAFF   There's neither honesty, manhood, nor good
        fellowship in thee, nor thou cam'st not of the blood
137   royal if thou darest not stand for ten shillings.

138 PRINCE   Well then, once in my days I'll be a madcap.

       FALSTAFF   Why, that's well said.

140 PRINCE   Well, come what will, I'll tarry at home.

       FALSTAFF   By the Lord, I'll be a traitor then, when thou
        art king.

       PRINCE   I care not.

       POINS   Sir John, I prithee, leave the prince and me alone.
        I will lay him down such reasons for this adventure that
        he shall go.

       FALSTAFF   Well, God give thee the spirit of persuasion
148   and him the ears of profiting, that what thou speakest
149   may move and what he hears may be believed, that the
150   true prince may (for recreation sake) prove a false thief;
151   for the poor abuses of the time want countenance.
        Farewell; you shall find me in Eastcheap.

153 PRINCE   Farewell, thou latter spring! farewell, All-
        hallow summer!   *[Exit Falstaff.]*

       POINS   Now, my good sweet honey lord, ride with us to-
        morrow. I have a jest to execute that I cannot manage

---

126 *bespoke* ordered   127 *Eastcheap* unsavory district of London; *it* i.e., the robbery   129 *tarry* stay   130 *Yedward* nickname of (Edward) Poins   132 *chops* fat cheeks, jaws   133 *make one* be one of the party   137 *stand for* (1) fight for, (2) be good for 10 shillings (value of a "royal," a denomination of coin)   138 *madcap* reckless one   148 *profiting* i.e., of persuasion   149 *move* i.e., move him   151 *countenance* encouragement   153 *latter spring* overgrown youth   153–54 *Allhallown summer* Indian summer

alone. Falstaff, Bardolph, Peto, and Gadshill shall rob
those men that we have already waylaid; yourself and I
will not be there; and when they have the booty, if you
and I do not rob them, cut this head off from my   *160*
shoulders.

PRINCE   How shall we part with them in setting forth?

POINS   Why, we will set forth before or after them and
appoint them a place of meeting, wherein it is at our
pleasure to fail; and then will they adventure upon the   *165*
exploit themselves, which they shall have no sooner
achieved, but we'll set upon them.

PRINCE   Yea, but 'tis like that they will know us by our
horses, by our habits, and by every other appointment,   *169*
to be ourselves.   *170*

POINS   Tut! our horses they shall not see – I'll tie them in
the wood; our vizards we will change after we leave
them; and, sirrah, I have cases of buckram for the
nonce, to immask our noted outward garments.   *174*

PRINCE   Yea, but I doubt they will be too hard for us.   *175*

POINS   Well, for two of them, I know them to be as true-
bred cowards as ever turned back; and for the third, if   *177*
he fight longer than he sees reason, I'll forswear arms.   *178*
The virtue of this jest will be the incomprehensible lies   *179*
that this same fat rogue will tell us when we meet at   *180*
supper: how thirty, at least, he fought with; what wards,   *181*
what blows, what extremities he endured; and in the re-   *182*
proof of this lives the jest.

PRINCE   Well, I'll go with thee. Provide us all things necessary and meet me tomorrow night in Eastcheap.
There I'll sup. Farewell.   *186*

POINS   Farewell, my lord.   *Exit.*

---

165 *to fail* to not show up; *adventure* undertake   169 *habits* clothes; *ap-*
pointment detail of appearance   174 *nonce* this purpose; *noted* known   175
doubt fear; *hard* much   177 *turned back* turned their backs and ran   178
forswear swear to give up   179 *incomprehensible* unbelievable, unlimited
181 *wards* parries (with a sword)   182 *extremities* hardships   182–83 *re-*
proof disproof   186 *sup* dine (eat supper)

PRINCE

188   I know you all, and will awhile uphold
      The unyoked humor of your idleness.
190   Yet herein will I imitate the sun,
191   Who doth permit the base contagious clouds
      To smother up his beauty from the world,
      That, when he please again to be himself,
194   Being wanted, he may be more wondered at
      By breaking through the foul and ugly mists
      Of vapors that did seem to strangle him.
197   If all the year were playing holidays,
198   To sport would be as tedious as to work;
      But when they seldom come, they wished-for come,
200   And nothing pleaseth but rare accidents.
201   So, when this loose behavior I throw off
      And pay the debt I never promisèd,
      By how much better than my word I am,
204   By so much shall I falsify men's hopes;
205   And, like bright metal on a sullen ground,
      My reformation, glitt'ring o'er my fault,
207   Shall show more goodly and attract more eyes
208   Than that which hath no foil to set it off.
209   I'll so offend to make offense a skill,
210   Redeeming time when men think least I will.   *Exit.*

*

188–89 *uphold . . . idleness* pretend to go along with the unrestrained mood of your frivolity   190 *herein* in this   191 *base contagious* low (with a suggestion of lower rank) and poisonous   194 *wanted* missed   197 *playing holidays* vacations   198 *sport* play   200 *rare accidents* unusual events   201 *loose* unruly, irresponsible   204 *By . . . hopes* I will greatly surprise expectations   205 *sullen* dark   207 *more goodly* to better advantage   208 *foil* contrasting background   209 *to* as to; *skill* clever strategy   210 *Redeeming time* making up for lost time

∿ **I.3** *Enter the King, Northumberland, Worcester,*
   Hotspur, Sir Walter Blunt, with others.

KING

My blood hath been too cold and temperate,
Unapt to stir at these indignities,   2
And you have found me, for accordingly   3
You tread upon my patience; but be sure
I will from henceforth rather be myself,   5
Mighty and to be feared, than my condition,   6
Which hath been smooth as oil, soft as young down,   7
And therefore lost that title of respect
Which the proud soul ne'er pays but to the proud.

WORCESTER

Our house, my sovereign liege, little deserves   10
The scourge of greatness to be used on it –   11
And that same greatness too which our own hands
Have holp to make so portly.   13

NORTHUMBERLAND

My lord –

KING

Worcester, get thee gone, for I do see
Danger and disobedience in thine eye.
O, sir, your presence is too bold and peremptory,
And majesty might never yet endure
The moody frontier of a servant brow.   19
You have good leave to leave us: when we need   20
Your use and counsel, we shall send for you.
                                             Exit Worcester.
You were about to speak.

NORTHUMBERLAND   Yea, my good lord.

I.3 The court   2 *indignities* offenses   3 *found me* found me to be so   5 *myself* i.e., kingly   6 *condition* i.e., mild temper   7 *down* soft goose feathers,
used for filling cushions   10 *house* family, clan   11 *scourge* punishment   13
holp helped; *portly* great (Worcester implies that his family helped Henry to
his throne)   19 *moody frontier* i.e., angry brow, forehead ("frontier" literally
means fortification); *servant* i.e., subservient   20 *good leave* permission

Those prisoners in your highness' name demanded
Which Harry Percy here at Holmedon took,
25 Were, as he says, not with such strength denied
26 As is deliverèd to your majesty.
27 Either envy, therefore, or misprision
Is guilty of this fault, and not my son.

HOTSPUR
My liege, I did deny no prisoners.
30 But I remember, when the fight was done,
When I was dry with rage and extreme toil,
Breathless and faint, leaning upon my sword,
Came there a certain lord, neat and trimly dressed,
34 Fresh as a bridegroom, and his chin new reaped
Showed like a stubble land at harvest home.
36 He was perfumèd like a milliner,
And 'twixt his finger and his thumb he held
38 A pouncet box, which ever and anon
He gave his nose, and took't away again;
40 Who therewith angry, when it next came there,
41 Took it in snuff; and still he smiled and talked;
And as the soldiers bore dead bodies by,
He called them untaught knaves, unmannerly,
To bring a slovenly unhandsome corpse
Betwixt the wind and his nobility.
46 With many holiday and lady terms
47 He questioned me, amongst the rest demanded
My prisoners in your majesty's behalf.
I then, all smarting with my wounds being cold,
50 To be so pestered with a popinjay,
Out of my grief and my impatience

---

25 *strength* i.e., vehemence   **26** *deliverèd* reported   **27** *misprision* mistake
34 *new reaped* i.e., freshly (and perhaps fashionably) shaven   **36** *milliner* one
who sells fashionable gloves and hats   **38** *pouncet box* perfumed box (sniffed
to mask unpleasant odors); *ever and anon* now and again   **40** *Who* i.e., his
nose   **41** *Took it* (1) inhaled it, (2) took offense (at the removal of the per-
fume)   **46** *holiday and lady* elegant and effeminate   **47** *questioned* (1) inter-
rogated, (2) kept on talking to; *amongst the rest* in the middle of which   **50**
popinjay parrot

Answered neglectingly, I know not what –   52
He should, or he should not; for he made me mad
To see him shine so brisk, and smell so sweet,
And talk so like a waiting gentlewoman
Of guns and drums and wounds – God save the mark! –   56
And telling me the sovereignest thing on earth   57
Was parmacety for an inward bruise,   58
And that it was great pity, so it was,
This villainous saltpeter should be digged   60
Out of the bowels of the harmless earth,   61
Which many a good tall fellow had destroyed
So cowardly, and but for these vile guns,
He would himself have been a soldier.
This bald unjointed chat of his, my lord,   65
I answered indirectly, as I said,
And I beseech you, let not his report
Come current for an accusation   68
Betwixt my love and your high majesty.

BLUNT
The circumstance considered, good my lord,   70
Whate'er Lord Harry Percy then had said
To such a person, and in such a place,
At such a time, with all the rest retold,
May reasonably die, and never rise
To do him wrong, or any way impeach   75
What then he said, so he unsay it now.

KING
Why, yet he doth deny his prisoners,   77
But with proviso and exception,   78
That we at our own charge shall ransom straight   79
His brother-in-law, the foolish Mortimer;   80

---

52 *neglectingly* carelessly   56 *God . . . mark!* God forbid!   57 *sovereignest*
most effective   58 *parmacety* spermaceti, an oily ointment derived from the
sperm whale, thought to have curative properties   60 *saltpeter* potassium ni-
trate, mined to make gunpowder   61 *bowels* inmost parts   65 *bald unjointed* frivolous and aimless   68 *Come current* stand as, be taken for   75 *do
him wrong* harm him; *impeach* discredit   77 *deny* deny me   78 *proviso and
exception* qualification, stipulations   79 *charge* expense; *straight* immediately

Who, on my soul, hath willfully betrayed
The lives of those that he did lead to fight
Against that great magician, damned Glendower,
84 Whose daughter, as we hear, that Earl of March
85 Hath lately married. Shall our coffers, then,
Be emptied to redeem a traitor home?
87 Shall we buy treason? and indent with fears
When they have lost and forfeited themselves?
No, on the barren mountains let him starve!
90 For I shall never hold that man my friend
Whose tongue shall ask me for one penny cost
92 To ransom home revolted Mortimer.

HOTSPUR
Revolted Mortimer?
94 He never did fall off, my sovereign liege,
But by the chance of war. To prove that true
Needs no more but one tongue for all those wounds,
97 Those mouthèd wounds, which valiantly he took
98 When on the gentle Severn's sedgy bank,
In single opposition hand to hand,
100 He did confound the best part of an hour
101 In changing hardiment with great Glendower.
102 Three times, they breathed, and three times did they drink,
Upon agreement, of swift Severn's flood;
Who then, affrighted with their bloody looks,
Ran fearfully among the trembling reeds
106 And hid his crisp head in the hollow bank,
Bloodstainèd with these valiant combatants.
108 Never did bare and rotten policy
109 Color her working with such deadly wounds;
110 Nor never could the noble Mortimer
Receive so many, and all willingly.

---

84 *that Earl of March* i.e., Mortimer   85 *coffers* treasure chests   87 *indent with fears* bargain with potential traitors, cowards   92 *revolted* rebellious   94 *fall off* betray loyalty   97 *mouthèd* gaping (as if to speak)   98 *Severn* river border of England and Wales; *sedgy* weed-covered   100 *confound* spend, use   101 *changing hardiment* exchanging blows   102 *breathed* paused, rested   106 *his* i.e., Severn's   108 *policy* statecraft   109 *Color* disguise

Then let not him be slandered with revolt.

KING

Thou dost belie him, Percy, thou dost belie him!   113
He never did encounter with Glendower.   114
I tell thee
He durst as well have met the devil alone   116
As Owen Glendower for an enemy.
Art thou not ashamed? But, sirrah, henceforth
Let me not hear you speak of Mortimer.
Send me your prisoners with the speediest means,   120
Or you shall hear in such a kind from me
As will displease you. My Lord Northumberland,
We license your departure with your son. –   123
Send us your prisoners, or you will hear of it.
                    Exeunt King [, Blunt, and train].

HOTSPUR

An if the devil come and roar for them,
I will not send them. I will after straight   126
And tell him so; for I will ease my heart,
Albeit I make a hazard of my head.   128

NORTHUMBERLAND

What, drunk with choler? Stay, and pause awhile.   129
Here comes your uncle.   130
    Enter Worcester.

HOTSPUR   Speak of Mortimer?
Zounds, I will speak of him, and let my soul
Want mercy if I do not join with him!   132
Yea, on his part I'll empty all these veins,
And shed my dear blood drop by drop in the dust,
But I will lift the downtrod Mortimer
As high in the air as this unthankful king,
As this ingrate and cankered Bolingbroke.   137

---

113 *belie* tell lies about   114 *encounter with* fight with   116 *durst* would
have dared   120 *with . . . means* in the speediest fashion   123 *license* sanc-
tion, permit   126 *will after straight* will go to him immediately   128 *Albeit . . . hazard of* even if I jeopardize   129 *choler* anger   132 *Want mercy* be
damned   137 *ingrate and cankered* ungrateful and corrupt; *Bolingbroke* the
name of Henry IV prior to his ascent of the throne

NORTHUMBERLAND
  Brother, the king hath made your nephew mad.
WORCESTER
  Who struck this heat up after I was gone?
HOTSPUR
140 He will (forsooth) have all my prisoners;
  And when I urged the ransom once again
  Of my wife's brother, then his cheek looked pale,
143 And on my face he turned an eye of death,
  Trembling even at the name of Mortimer.
WORCESTER
  I cannot blame him. Was not he proclaimed
146 By Richard that dead is, the next of blood?
NORTHUMBERLAND
  He was; I heard the proclamation.
  And then it was when the unhappy king
149 (Whose wrongs in us God pardon!) did set forth
150 Upon his Irish expedition;
151 From whence he intercepted did return
  To be deposed, and shortly murderèd.
WORCESTER
  And for whose death we in the world's wide mouth
154 Live scandalized and foully spoken of.
HOTSPUR
155 But soft, I pray you. Did King Richard then
156 Proclaim my brother Edmund Mortimer
  Heir to the crown?
NORTHUMBERLAND He did; myself did hear it.
HOTSPUR
158 Nay, then I cannot blame his cousin king,
159 That wished him on the barren mountains starve.
160 But shall it be that you, that set the crown

---

143 *of death* of deadly fear   146 *Richard* Richard II, the previous king, murdered by order of Henry IV   149 *wrongs in us* harms we caused   150 *Irish expedition* wars in Ireland   151 *whence . . . intercepted* where he was called back   154 *scandalized* covered with scandal (for helping to depose)   155 *soft* wait a minute   156 *brother* brother-in-law   158 *cousin* with a pun on "cozen," to cheat   159 *barren mountains* i.e., in Wales

Upon the head of this forgetful man,
And for his sake wear the detested blot
Of murderous subornation – shall it be   163
That you a world of curses undergo,
Being the agents or base second means,   165
The cords, the ladder, or the hangman rather?
O, pardon me that I descend so low
To show the line and the predicament   168
Wherein you range under this subtle king!   169
Shall it for shame be spoken in these days,   170
Or fill up chronicles in time to come,   171
That men of your nobility and power
Did gage them both in an unjust behalf   173
(As both of you, God pardon it! have done)
To put down Richard, that sweet lovely rose,
And plant this thorn, this canker, Bolingbroke?   176
And shall it in more shame be further spoken
That you are fooled, discarded, and shook off
By him for whom these shames ye underwent?
No! yet time serves wherein you may redeem   180
Your banished honors and restore yourselves
Into the good thoughts of the world again;
Revenge the jeering and disdained contempt   183
Of this proud king, who studies day and night
To answer all the debt he owes to you   185
Even with the bloody payment of your deaths.
Therefore I say –
WORCESTER   Peace, cousin, say no more;
And now I will unclasp a secret book,   188
And to your quick-conceiving discontents   189
I'll read you matter deep and dangerous,   190

---

163 *murderous subornation* urging him to murder Richard II   165 *base second means* agents   168 *line* connection (with the crime), station   169 *range* are situated; *subtle* devious   171 *chronicles* histories   173 *gage* pledge themselves; *behalf* cause   176 *canker* (1) wild rose, (2) ulcer   180–81 *redeem . . . honors* reclaim your lost reputation   183 *disdained* disdainful   185 *answer* repay   188 *secret book* plan   189 *quick-conceiving discontents* quick-witted grievances

As full of peril and adventurous spirit
As to o'erwalk a current roaring loud
193   On the unsteadfast footing of a spear.
HOTSPUR
194   If he fall in, good night, or sink or swim!
Send danger from the east unto the west,
196   So honor cross it from the north to south,
And let them grapple. O, the blood more stirs
To rouse a lion than to start a hare!
NORTHUMBERLAND
Imagination of some great exploit
200   Drives him beyond the bounds of patience.
HOTSPUR
By heaven, methinks it were an easy leap
202   To pluck bright honor from the pale-faced moon,
203   Or dive into the bottom of the deep,
204   Where fathom line could never touch the ground,
205   And pluck up drownèd honor by the locks,
206   So he that doth redeem her thence might wear
207   Without corrival all her dignities;
208   But out upon this half-faced fellowship!
WORCESTER
209   He apprehends a world of figures here,
210   But not the form of what he should attend.
211   Good cousin, give me audience for a while.
HOTSPUR
212   I cry you mercy.
WORCESTER   Those same noble Scots
That are your prisoners —
HOTSPUR   I'll keep them all.

---

193 *spear* (spear laid over rushing water) 194 *or* whether he 196 *So* so
long as, in order that 200 *him* i.e., Hotspur 202 *moon* a symbol of
chastity 203 *deep* ocean 204 *fathom line* a weighted line marked every six
feet (a fathom), used to measure water 205 *locks* hair 206 *her thence* her
(honor) from there 207 *corrival* partner, rival 208 *half-faced fellowship*
sharing of honors 209 *figures* figures of imagination, or of speech 210 *attend* pay attention to 211 *give me audience* let me speak; listen to me 212
cry you mercy beg your pardon

By God, he shall not have a Scot of them!   214
No, if a Scot would save his soul, he shall not.
I'll keep them, by this hand!   216

WORCESTER   You start away
And lend no ear unto my purposes.
Those prisoners you shall keep.

HOTSPUR   Nay, I will! That's flat!
He said he would not ransom Mortimer,
Forbade my tongue to speak of Mortimer,   220
But I will find him when he lies asleep,
And in his ear I'll hollow "Mortimer."
Nay, I'll have a starling shall be taught to speak
Nothing but "Mortimer," and give it him
To keep his anger still in motion.   225

WORCESTER
Hear you, cousin, a word.

HOTSPUR
All studies here I solemnly defy   227
Save how to gall and pinch this Bolingbroke;   228
And that same sword-and-buckler Prince of Wales: 229
But that I think his father loves him not   230
And would be glad he met with some mischance,
I would have him poisoned with a pot of ale.

WORCESTER
Farewell, kinsman. I will talk to you
When you are better tempered to attend.   234

NORTHUMBERLAND
Why, what a wasp-stung and impatient fool
Art thou to break into this woman's mood,   236
Tying thine ear to no tongue but thine own!

HOTSPUR
Why, look you, I am whipped and scourged with rods,   238

---

214 *a Scot* a small amount   216 *start away* jump into your own train of
thought   225 *still* ever, constantly   227 *studies* pursuits, interests; *defy* renounce   228 *gall* make sore   229 *buckler* small round shield (i.e., improp-
erly, basely armed; princes should carry rapiers and daggers)   230 *But that* if
it weren't that   234 *tempered* disposed, self-controlled   236 *woman's mood*
quarrelsome, shrewish, or talkative mood   238 *scourged* whipped

239   Nettled, and stung with pismires when I hear
240   Of this vile politician, Bolingbroke.
        In Richard's time – what do you call the place?
        A plague upon it! it is in Gloucestershire;
243   'Twas where the madcap duke his uncle kept,
        His uncle York – where I first bowed my knee
        Unto this king of smiles, this Bolingbroke –
246   'Sblood! – when you and he came back from Ravens-
            purgh –
NORTHUMBERLAND
247   At Berkeley Castle.
HOTSPUR
        You say true.
249   Why, what a candy deal of courtesy
250   This fawning greyhound then did proffer me!
251   "Look when his infant fortune came to age,"
        And "gentle Harry Percy," and "kind cousin" –
253   O, the devil take such cozeners! – God forgive me!
        Good uncle, tell your tale, for I have done.
WORCESTER
        Nay, if you have not, to it again.
256   We will stay your leisure.
HOTSPUR   I have done, i' faith.
WORCESTER
        Then once more to your Scottish prisoners.
        Deliver them up without their ransom straight,
259   And make the Douglas' son your only mean
260   For powers in Scotland – which, for divers reasons
        Which I shall send you written, be assured
        Will easily be granted.

---

239 *Nettled* stung as if by thorns of the nettle plant; *pismires* ants 240
politician one given to policy or cunning statecraft 243 *kept* dwelled 246
Ravenspurgh a port at the mouth of River Humber in Yorkshire (now under
water) where Bolingbroke reentered England upon his return from exile
247 *Berkeley Castle* castle near Bristol 249 *candy deal* sugary amount 250
fawning greyhound flattering house pet 251 *"Look . . . age"* as soon as his
promise matured 253 *cozeners* cheaters 256 *stay* wait for 259 *the Douglas' son* i.e., Mordake (Murdoch); *mean* agent 260 *divers* several

[To Northumberland] You, my lord,
Your son in Scotland being thus employed,
Shall secretly into the bosom creep   264
Of that same noble prelate well-beloved,
The archbishop.

HOTSPUR   Of York, is it not?

WORCESTER
True; who bears hard   267
His brother's death at Bristow, the Lord Scroop.
I speak not this in estimation,   269
As what I think might be, but what I know   *270*
Is ruminated, plotted, and set down,
And only stays but to behold the face   272
Of that occasion that shall bring it on.

HOTSPUR
I smell it. Upon my life, it will do well.

NORTHUMBERLAND
Before the game is afoot thou still let'st slip.   275

HOTSPUR
Why, it cannot choose but be a noble plot.
And then the power of Scotland and of York
To join with Mortimer, ha?

WORCESTER   And so they shall.

HOTSPUR
In faith, it is exceedingly well aimed.

WORCESTER
And 'tis no little reason bids us speed   *280*
To save our heads by raising of a head;   281
For, bear ourselves as even as we can,   282
The king will always think him in our debt,
And think we think ourselves unsatisfied,
Till he hath found a time to pay us home.   285
And see already how he doth begin

---

264 *bosom* confidence 267 *bears hard* resents, begrudges 269 *in estimation* by guessing 272–73 *And . . . on* and waits only for the sign of its opportunity to begin 275 *let'st slip* i.e., release the dogs of war (i.e., you're
ready to start fighting even before the plan is in place) 281 *a head* army,
force 282 *as even* as carefully 285 *home* completely (i.e., kill us)

To make us strangers to his looks of love.

HOTSPUR
He does, he does! We'll be revenged on him.

WORCESTER
Cousin, farewell. No further go in this
290 Than I by letters shall direct your course.
291 When time is ripe, which will be suddenly,
292 I'll steal to Glendower and Lord Mortimer,
Where you and Douglas, and our pow'rs at once,
294 As I will fashion it, shall happily meet,
To bear our fortunes in our own strong arms,
296 Which now we hold at much uncertainty.

NORTHUMBERLAND
Farewell, good brother. We shall thrive, I trust.

HOTSPUR
Uncle, adieu. O, let the hours be short
Till fields and blows and groans applaud our sport!
Exeunt.

*

❧ **II.1** *Enter a Carrier with a lantern in his hand.*

1 FIRST CARRIER Heigh-ho! an it be not four by the day,
2   I'll be hanged. Charles' wain is over the new chimney,
3   and yet our horse not packed. – What, ostler!
4 OSTLER *[Within]* Anon, anon.
5 FIRST CARRIER I prithee, Tom, beat Cut's saddle, put a
6   few flocks in the point. Poor jade is wrung in the with-
7   ers out of all cess.

---

291 *suddenly* soon **292** *steal to* go secretly to **294** *fashion* plan **296**
Which i.e., our fortunes
    II.1 A stable yard of an inn on the road between London and Canterbury
1 *by the day* in the morning **2** *Charles' wain* Charlemagne's wagon, or the
constellation Ursa Major (the Big Dipper) **3** *yet* still; *horse* horses; *ostler*
(from hostler), one who handles horses **4** *Anon* in a minute; be right there
5 *beat* soften **6** *flocks* sheepskin tufts; *point* pommel of the saddle, the part
that covers the horse's withers (the highest point of the shoulder at the base
of the neck); *jade* nag; *wrung in* sore at **7** *out . . . cess* beyond all measure

Enter another Carrier.

SECOND CARRIER   Peas and beans are as dank here as a   8
dog, and that is the next way to give poor jades the   9
bots. This house is turned upside down since Robin   10
Ostler died.

FIRST CARRIER   Poor fellow never joyed since the price of
oats rose. It was the death of him.

SECOND CARRIER   I think this be the most villainous   14
house in all London road for fleas. I am stung like a
tench.   16

FIRST CARRIER   Like a tench? By the mass, there is ne'er a
king christen could be better bit than I have been since   18
the first cock.   19

SECOND CARRIER   Why, they will allow us ne'er a jordan,   20
and then we leak in your chimney, and your chamber   21
lye breeds fleas like a loach.   22

FIRST CARRIER   What, ostler! come away and be hanged!   23
come away!

SECOND CARRIER   I have a gammon of bacon and two   25
razes of ginger, to be delivered as far as Charing Cross.   26

FIRST CARRIER   God's body! the turkeys in my pannier   27
are quite starved. What, ostler! A plague on thee! hast
thou never an eye in thy head? Canst not hear? An
'twere not as good deed as drink to break the pate on   30
thee, I am a very villain. Come, and be hanged! Hast   31
no faith in thee?

Enter Gadshill.

GADSHILL   Good morrow, carriers. What's o'clock?

FIRST CARRIER   I think it be two o'clock.

---

8 *Peas and beans* horse feed   8–9 *dank . . . dog* very wet   9 *next* quickest
10 *bots* worms   14 *most villainous* worst (most evil)   16 *tench* a red spotted
fish   18 *king christen* Christian king   19 *first cock* midnight   20 *jordan* chamber pot   21 *leak in your chimney* piss in the fireplace   21–22 *chamber lye* urine
(lye is a caustic alkaline solution)   22 *loach* a small freshwater fish   23 *come
away and be hanged* come here or be hanged   25 *gammon* a ham, or side of
bacon   26 *razes* roots; *Charing Cross* a market town lying between London
and Westminster   27 *pannier* saddlebag or basket   30–31 *to . . . thee* to hit
you on the head   31–32 *Hast . . . thee?* Are you completely unreliable?

GADSHILL   I prithee lend me thy lantern to see my gelding in the stable.

37 FIRST CARRIER   Nay, by God, soft! I know a trick worth
two of that, i' faith.

GADSHILL   I pray thee lend me thine.

40 SECOND CARRIER   Ay, when? canst tell? Lend me thy
lantern, quoth he? Marry, I'll see thee hanged first!

42 GADSHILL   Sirrah carrier, what time do you mean to
come to London?

SECOND CARRIER   Time enough to go to bed with a can-
45 dle, I warrant thee. Come, neighbor Mugs, we'll call up
46 the gentlemen. They will along with company, for they
47 have great charge.   *Exeunt [Carriers].*

48 GADSHILL   What, ho! chamberlain!
Enter Chamberlain.

49 CHAMBERLAIN   At hand, quoth pickpurse.

50 GADSHILL   That's even as fair as "at hand, quoth the
51 chamberlain"; for thou variest no more from picking of
purses than giving direction doth from laboring: thou
layest the plot how.

54 CHAMBERLAIN   Good morrow, Master Gadshill. It holds
55 current that I told you yesternight. There's a franklin in
56 the Weald of Kent hath brought three hundred marks
57 with him in gold. I heard him tell it to one of his company last night at supper – a kind of auditor, one that
59 hath abundance of charge too, God knows what. They
60 are up already and call for eggs and butter. They will
61 away presently.

---

37 *soft* hold on, wait   40 *Ay . . . tell* i.e., never   42 *Sirrah* mister   45 *war-rant thee* guarantee you   46 *will along* will go   47 *great charge* valuable lug-gage   48 *chamberlain* male equivalent of a chambermaid   49 *At . . . pickpurse* I'm right beside you, as the pickpurse said   50 *as fair as* to say   51–53 *thou . . . how* you differ no more from a pickpurse than giving orders does from laboring – i.e., you show how it's done   54–55 *holds current that* is still true what   55 *franklin* a small farmer who owns his own land   56 *Weald* forest; *marks* coins worth 13 shillings 4 pence   57–58 *company* com-panions   59 *abundance of charge* valuable goods   61 *presently* at once

GADSHILL   Sirrah, if they meet not with Saint Nicholas'   62
  clerks, I'll give thee this neck.
CHAMBERLAIN   No, I'll none of it. I pray thee keep that
  for the hangman; for I know thou worshippest Saint
  Nicholas as truly as a man of falsehood may.
GADSHILL   What talkest thou to me of the hangman? If I
  hang, I'll make a fat pair of gallows; for if I hang, old Sir
  John hangs with me, and thou knowest he is no
  starveling. Tut! there are other Troyans that thou dream'st   70
  not of, the which for sport sake are content to do the pro-   71
  fession some grace; that would (if matters should be   72
  looked into) for their own credit sake make all whole. I   73
  am joined with no foot landrakers, no long-staff six-   74
  penny strikers, none of these mad mustachio purple-   75
  hued maltworms; but with nobility and tranquillity,   76
  burgomasters and great oneyers, such as can hold in, such   77
  as will strike sooner than speak, and speak sooner than   78
  drink, and drink sooner than pray; and yet, zounds, I lie;
  for they pray continually to their saint, the common-   80
  wealth, or rather, not pray to her, but prey on her, for
  they ride up and down on her and make her their boots.   82
CHAMBERLAIN   What, the commonwealth their boots?
  Will she hold out water in foul way?   84
GADSHILL   She will, she will! Justice hath liquored her.   85
  We steal as in a castle, cocksure. We have the receipt of   86
  fern seed, we walk invisible.   87

62–63 *St. Nicholas' clerks* highwaymen (Saint Nicholas was the patron saint of
thieves; clerks are monks or clerics)   **70** *starveling* thin man; *Troyans* play-
boys, sports   **71** *sport* fun's   **71–72** *the profession* i.e., of thieving   **72** *grace*
credit   **73** *looked into* investigated   **73** *make all whole* repair any damage
74 *foot landrakers* footpads, thugs   **74–75** *long-staff sixpenny strikers* robbers
with long staffs (a peasant's weapon) who knock down victims for a small
amount of money   **75–76** *mustachio . . . maltworms* drunkards with beer-
stained mustaches   **76** *tranquillity* those with an easy life   **77** *burgomasters*
respectable citizens (chief magistrates); *great oneyers* great ones; *hold in* keep
secret   **78** *speak* i.e., say "hands up!"   **82** *boots* booty   **84** *in foul way* in a
bad road   **85** *liquored her* greased her, lubricated her (bribed)   **86** *as . . . castle* in safety; *receipt* recipe   **87** *fern seed* (thought because of its own virtual in-
visibility to confer it)

88 CHAMBERLAIN Nay, by my faith, I think you are more
beholding to the night than to fern seed for your walk-
90 ing invisible.

GADSHILL Give me thy hand. Thou shalt have a share in
92 our purchase, as I am a true man.

93 CHAMBERLAIN Nay, rather let me have it, as you are a
94 false thief.

95 GADSHILL Go to; "homo" is a common name to all men.
Bid the ostler bring my gelding out of the stable.
97 Farewell, you muddy knave.   *[Exeunt.]*

*

⸎ **II.2** *Enter Prince, Poins, Peto [and Bardolph].*

1 POINS Come, shelter, shelter! I have removed Falstaff's
2 horse, and he frets like a gummed velvet.

3 PRINCE Stand close.   *[They step aside.]*
Enter Falstaff.

FALSTAFF Poins! Poins, and be hanged! Poins!

PRINCE *[Comes forward.]* Peace, ye fat-kidneyed rascal!
6 What a brawling dost thou keep!

FALSTAFF Where's Poins, Hal?

PRINCE He is walked up to the top of the hill; I'll go seek
him.   *[Steps aside.]*

10 FALSTAFF I am accursed to rob in that thieve's company.
The rascal hath removed my horse and tied him I know
12 not where. If I travel but four foot by the squire further
13 afoot, I shall break my wind. Well, I doubt not but to die
a fair death for all this, if I scape hanging for killing that
rogue. I have forsworn his company hourly any time this
two-and-twenty years, and yet I am bewitched with the

88–89 *are . . . to* owe more to   **92** *purchase* takings, loot   **93** *it* all of it   **94**
false pretend   **95** *homo* Latin for "man"   **97** *muddy* stupid
  II.2 On the road at Gad's Hill   **1** *shelter* hide   **2** *frets* chafes; *gummed velvet* velvet made rigid with gum and liable to wear (a horse easily spooked)
3 *close* aside   **6** *keep* make, keep up   **10** *thieve's* thief's   **12** *squire* a measur-
ing instrument   **13** *break my wind* be totally out of breath (with scatological
innuendo)

rogue's company. If the rascal have not given me medi- 17
cines to make me love him, I'll be hanged. It could not be
else: I have drunk medicines. Poins! Hal! A plague upon
you both! Bardolph! Peto! I'll starve ere I'll rob a foot fur- 20
ther. An 'twere not as good a deed as drink to turn true 21
man and to leave these rogues, I am the veriest varlet that 22
ever chewed with a tooth. Eight yards of uneven ground
is threescore and ten miles afoot with me, and the stony- 24
hearted villains know it well enough. A plague upon it
when thieves cannot be true one to another! *(They whis-*
tle.) Whew! A plague upon you all! Give me my horse, 27
you rogues! give me my horse and be hanged!

PRINCE *[Comes forward.]* Peace, ye fat-guts! Lie down,
lay thine ear close to the ground, and list if thou canst 30
hear the tread of travelers. 31

FALSTAFF   Have you any levers to lift me up again, being
down? 'Sblood, I'll not bear mine own flesh so far afoot
again for all the coin in thy father's exchequer. What a 34
plague mean ye to colt me thus? 35

PRINCE   Thou liest; thou art not colted, thou art un-
colted.

FALSTAFF   I prithee, good Prince Hal, help me to my
horse, good king's son.

PRINCE   Out, ye rogue! Shall I be your ostler? 40

FALSTAFF   Go hang thyself in thine own heir-apparent
garters! If I be ta'en, I'll peach for this. An I have not 42
ballads made on you all, and sung to filthy tunes, let a
cup of sack be my poison. When a jest is so forward – 44
and afoot too – I hate it. 45

   Enter Gadshill.

17–18 *medicines* love potions   21 *true* honest   22 *veriest varlet* truest knave,
rascal   24 *threescore and ten* seventy   27 *Whew!* (Falstaff either whistles in
reply, mockingly, or gasps for breath)   30 *list* listen   31 *tread* footfalls   34
exchequer treasury   35 *colt* trick (as by a young unruly horse)   40 *Out* get
out of here   42 *garters* straps that hold up stockings (with mocking reference
to the Order of the Garter, a brotherhood of knights); *peach* squeal, inform
44 *so forward* so out of control; so far advanced   45 *afoot* i.e., not on horse-
back

GADSHILL Stand!

FALSTAFF So I do, against my will.

48 POINS *[Comes forward.]* O, 'tis our setter; I know his voice.

50 BARDOLPH What news?

51 GADSHILL Case ye, case ye! On with your vizards! There's money of the king's coming down the hill; 'tis going to the king's exchequer.

FALSTAFF You lie, ye rogue! 'Tis going to the king's tavern.

55 GADSHILL There's enough to make us all.

FALSTAFF To be hanged.

57 PRINCE Sirs, you four shall front them in the narrow lane; Ned Poins and I will walk lower. If they scape
59 from your encounter, then they light on us.

60 PETO How many be there of them?

GADSHILL Some eight or ten.

FALSTAFF Zounds, will they not rob us?

PRINCE What, a coward, Sir John Paunch?

64 FALSTAFF Indeed, I am not John of Gaunt, your grandfather, but yet no coward, Hal.

PRINCE Well, we leave that to the proof.

POINS Sirrah Jack, thy horse stands behind the hedge. When thou need'st him, there thou shalt find him. Farewell and stand fast.

70 FALSTAFF Now cannot I strike him, if I should be hanged.

PRINCE *[Aside to Poins]* Ned, where are our disguises?

POINS *[Aside to Prince]* Here, hard by. Stand close.

                [Exeunt Prince and Poins.]

74 FALSTAFF Now, my masters, happy man be his dole, say I. Every man to his business.

    Enter the Travelers.

TRAVELER Come, neighbor. The boy shall lead our

---

48 *setter* person who arranged the robbery **51** *Case ye* put on your masks
55 *make us* make our fortunes **57** *front* confront, accost **59** *light on* find
64 *Gaunt* with pun on "thin" **70** *cannot . . . him* I can't hit him **74**
happy . . . dole may all men find happiness

horses down the hill; we'll walk afoot awhile and ease
our legs.

THIEVES   Stand!

TRAVELER   Jesus bless us!   80

FALSTAFF   Strike! down with them! cut the villains'
throats! Ah, whoreson caterpillars! bacon-fed knaves!   82
they hate us youth. Down with them! fleece them!   83

TRAVELER   O, we are undone, both we and ours forever!   84

FALSTAFF   Hang ye, gorbellied knaves, are ye undone?   85
No, ye fat chuffs; I would your store were here! On, ba-   86
cons, on! What, ye knaves! young men must live. You
are grandjurors, are ye? We'll jure ye, faith!   88

> *Here they rob them and bind them. Exeunt.*
> *Enter the Prince and Poins [in buckram suits].*

PRINCE   The thieves have bound the true men. Now
could thou and I rob the thieves and go merrily to Lon-   90
don, it would be argument for a week, laughter for a
month, and a good jest forever.

POINS   Stand close! I hear them coming.

> *[They stand aside.]*
> *Enter the Thieves again.*

FALSTAFF   Come, my masters, let us share, and then to   94
horse before day. An the prince and Poins be not two
arrant cowards, there's no equity stirring. There's no   96
more valor in that Poins than in a wild duck.   97

PRINCE Your money! ⎰ *As they are sharing, the prince and*
⎱ *Poins set upon them. They all run*
away, and Falstaff, after a blow or
two, runs away too, leaving the
POINS Villains! ⎱ *booty behind them.*

PRINCE   Got with much ease. Now merrily to horse. The   100
thieves are all scattered, and possessed with fear so

---

82 *whoreson* son of a whore; *caterpillars* parasites; *bacon-fed* well-fed   83
fleece take all they have (as in shearing a sheep)   84 *undone* finished; *ours* our
families   85 *gorbellied* big-bellied   86 *chuffs* churls, misers   88 *grandjurors*
men of wealth, able to serve on juries   94 *share* divide the loot   96 *arrant*
out-and-out (with pun on "errant," as in wandering or runaway); *equity*
judgment   97 *wild duck* (notoriously timid)

strongly that they dare not meet each other: each takes
103   his fellow for an officer. Away, good Ned. Falstaff
104   sweats to death and lards the lean earth as he walks
along. Were't not for laughing, I should pity him.
POINS How the fat rogue roared!   *Exeunt.*

*

❧ **II.3** *Enter Hotspur [alone], reading a letter.*

HOTSPUR "But, for mine own part, my lord, I could be
2   well contented to be there, in respect of the love I bear
3   your house." He could be contented – why is he not
then? In respect of the love he bears our house! He
shows in this he loves his own barn better than he loves
our house. Let me see some more. "The purpose you
undertake is dangerous" – why, that's certain! 'Tis dangerous to take a cold, to sleep, to drink; but I tell you,
9   my lord fool, out of this nettle, danger, we pluck this
10   flower, safety. "The purpose you undertake is dangerous, the friends you have named uncertain, the time it-
12   self unsorted, and your whole plot too light for the
counterpoise of so great an opposition." Say you so, say
you so? I say unto you again, you are a shallow, cow-
15   ardly hind, and you lie. What a lackbrain is this! By the
Lord, our plot is a good plot as ever was laid; our
friends true and constant: a good plot, good friends,
18   and full of expectation; an excellent plot, very good
friends. What a frosty-spirited rogue is this! Why,
20   my Lord of York commends the plot and the general
21   course of the action. Zounds, an I were now by this rascal, I could brain him with his lady's fan. Is there not
my father, my uncle, and myself; Lord Edmund Mor-

---

103 *an officer* a constable 104 *lards* greases

    II.3 Hotspur's castle at Warkworth 2 *in respect of* on account of 3 *house*
family 9 *out of this nettle* (nettles are a prickly plant that must be grasped
firmly to be plucked safely) 12 *unsorted* unsuitable 12–13 *too . . . opposition* too flimsy to meet so numerous an enemy 15 *hind* peasant, rustic 18
expectation promise 21 *an . . . by* if I were with

timer, my Lord of York, and Owen Glendower? Is there
not, besides, the Douglas? Have I not all their letters to
meet me in arms by the ninth of the next month, and
are they not some of them set forward already? What a
pagan rascal is this! an infidel! Ha! you shall see now, in   28
very sincerity of fear and cold heart will he to the king
and lay open all our proceedings. O, I could divide my-   30
self and go to buffets for moving such a dish of skim   31
milk with so honorable an action! Hang him, let him
tell the king! we are prepared. I will set forward tonight.
    Enter his Lady.
How now, Kate? I must leave you within these two
hours.

LADY PERCY
    O my good lord, why are you thus alone?
    For what offense have I this fortnight been   37
    A banished woman from my Harry's bed?
    Tell me, sweet lord, what is't that takes from thee
    Thy stomach, pleasure, and thy golden sleep?   40
    Why dost thou bend thine eyes upon the earth,
    And start so often when thou sit'st alone?   42
    Why hast thou lost the fresh blood in thy cheeks
    And given my treasures and my rights of thee   44
    To thick-eyed musing and cursed melancholy?   45
    In thy faint slumbers I by thee have watched,
    And heard thee murmur tales of iron wars,
    Speak terms of manage to thy bounding steed,   48
    Cry "Courage! to the field!" And thou hast talked
    Of sallies and retires, of trenches, tents,   50
    Of palisadoes, frontiers, parapets,   51

---

28 *pagan* heretic, unbeliever   28 *infidel* pagan   30–31 *divide . . . buffets* fight
with myself   31 *moving* urging   37 *fortnight* two weeks   40 *stomach* appetite
42 *start* jump involuntarily   44 *treasures . . . thee* what I treasure and have a
right to own   45 *thick-eyed musing* vacant, dull-sighted thought   48 *terms of
manage* horsemanship commands   50 *sallies* attack from a defensive position; *retires* retreats   51 *palisadoes* stakes set in the ground for defense; *fron-
tiers* defensive position; *parapets* walls, ramparts

52 Of basilisks, of cannon, culverin,
Of prisoners' ransom, and of soldiers slain,
54 And all the currents of a heady fight.
Thy spirit within thee hath been so at war,
And thus hath so bestirred thee in thy sleep,
That beads of sweat have stood upon thy brow
Like bubbles in a late-disturbèd stream,
And in thy face strange motions have appeared,
60 Such as we see when men restrain their breath
61 On some great sudden hest. O, what portents are these?
62 Some heavy business hath my lord in hand,
And I must know it, else he loves me not.

HOTSPUR
What, ho!
    [Enter a Servant.]
            Is Gilliams with the packet gone?

SERVANT
He is, my lord, an hour ago.

HOTSPUR
Hath Butler brought those horses from the sheriff?

SERVANT
One horse, my lord, he brought even now.

HOTSPUR
68 What horse? A roan, a crop-ear, is it not?

SERVANT
It is, my lord.

HOTSPUR   That roan shall be my throne.
70 Well, I will back him straight. O Esperance!
Bid Butler lead him forth into the park. *[Exit Servant.]*

LADY PERCY
But hear you, my lord.

HOTSPUR
What say'st thou, my lady?

---

52 *basilisks* large cannon; *culverin* long cannon 54 *heady* headlong 61 *hest* command; *portents* signs, prophecies 62 *heavy* serious, sorrowful 68 *roan* usually a reddish horse (with red and white hairs mixed) 70 *back* mount; *Esperance* hope (Percy family motto)

LADY PERCY
    What is it carries you away?
HOTSPUR
    Why, my horse, my love – my horse!
LADY PERCY
    Out, you mad-headed ape!
    A weasel hath not such a deal of spleen   77
    As you are tossed with. In faith,   78
    I'll know your business, Harry; that I will!
    I fear my brother Mortimer doth stir   80
    About his title and hath sent for you   81
    To line his enterprise; but if you go –   82
HOTSPUR
    So far afoot, I shall be weary, love.
LADY PERCY
    Come, come, you paraquito, answer me   84
    Directly unto this question that I ask.
    In faith, I'll break thy little finger, Harry,
    An if thou wilt not tell me all things true.
HOTSPUR
    Away, away, you trifler! Love? I love thee not;   88
    I care not for thee, Kate. This is no world
    To play with mammets and to tilt with lips.   90
    We must have bloody noses and cracked crowns,   91
    And pass them current too. God's me, my horse!   92
    What say'st thou, Kate? What wouldst thou have with
        me?
LADY PERCY
    Do you not love me? do you not indeed?
    Well, do not then; for since you love me not,
    I will not love myself. Do you not love me?
    Nay, tell me if you speak in jest or no.

---

77 *spleen* (thought to be source of hasty and irritable behavior) 78 *tossed with* agitatedly moved by 80–81 *stir/About* make a move for 81 *title* claim to the throne 82 *line* strengthen 84 *paraquito* parrot 88 *trifler* frivolous person 90 *mammets* dolls; *tilt* joust 91 *crowns* (1) heads, (2) 5-shilling coins 92 *pass them current* spend them; *God's me* God save me

HOTSPUR
    Come, wilt thou see me ride?
    And when I am a-horseback, I will swear
100   I love thee infinitely. But hark you, Kate:
    I must not have you henceforth question me
    Whither I go, nor reason whereabout.
    Whither I must, I must, and to conclude,
    This evening must I leave you, gentle Kate.
    I know you wise, but yet no farther wise
106   Than Harry Percy's wife; constant you are,
    But yet a woman; and for secrecy,
108   No lady closer, for I well believe
    Thou wilt not utter what thou dost not know,
110   And so far will I trust thee, gentle Kate.

LADY PERCY
    How? so far?

HOTSPUR
    Not an inch further. But hark you, Kate:
    Whither I go, thither shall you go too;
    Today will I set forth, tomorrow you.
115   Will this content you, Kate?

LADY PERCY   It must of force.   *Exeunt.*

*

  ∾ **II.4** *Enter Prince and Poins.*

1 PRINCE   Ned, prithee come out of that fat room and lend
    me thy hand to laugh a little.

  POINS   Where hast been, Hal?

4 PRINCE   With three or four loggerheads amongst three or
5   fourscore hogsheads. I have sounded the very bass
6   string of humility. Sirrah, I am sworn brother to a leash

---

106 *constant* trustworthy   **108** *closer* more close-mouthed   **115** *of force* of necessity

   II.4 Eastcheap tavern   **1** *fat* stuffy (or filled with vats)   **4** *loggerheads* blockheads   **5** *hogsheads* barrels; *sounded* caused to sound (i.e., strummed), measured the depths of; *bass* with pun on "base," lowborn   **6** *leash* three

of drawers and can call them all by their christen 7
names, as Tom, Dick, and Francis. They take it already
upon their salvation that, though I be but Prince of 9
Wales, yet I am the king of courtesy, and tell me flatly I 10
am no proud Jack like Falstaff, but a Corinthian, a lad 11
of mettle, a good boy (by the Lord, so they call me!), 12
and when I am King of England I shall command all
the good lads in Eastcheap. They call drinking deep,
dyeing scarlet; and when you breathe in your watering, 15
they cry "hem!" and bid you play it off. To conclude, I 16
am so good a proficient in one quarter of an hour that I 17
can drink with any tinker in his own language during 18
my life. I tell thee, Ned, thou hast lost much honor that
thou wert not with me in this action. But, sweet Ned – 20
to sweeten which name of Ned, I give thee this pennyworth of sugar, clapped even now into my hand by an
underskinker, one that never spake other English in his 23
life than "Eight shillings and sixpence," and "You are
welcome," with this shrill addition, "Anon, anon, sir! 25
Score a pint of bastard in the Half-moon," or so   but, 26
Ned, to drive away the time till Falstaff come, I prithee
do thou stand in some by-room while I question my 28
puny drawer to what end he gave me the sugar; and do 29
thou never leave calling "Francis!" that his tale to me 30
may be nothing but "Anon!" Step aside, and I'll show
thee a precedent. 32

POINS   Francis!
PRINCE   Thou art perfect.
POINS   Francis!   *[Exit Poins.]*

---

7 *drawers* waiters; *christen* Christian (i.e., first, as opposed to family name)
9 *upon their salvation* as they hope to be eternally saved (as in swearing upon)
11 *Corinthian* good sport   12 *mettle* courage   15 *scarlet* dyes were best fixed
with drunkards' urine (i.e., of high alcohol content); *breathe* pause; *watering*
drinking   16 *play it off* drink up   17 *a proficient* an expert   18 *tinker*
vagabond, Gypsy   23 *underskinker* bartender's assistant   25 *Anon* Coming!
Be right there   26 *Score* charge; *bastard* sweet Spanish wine; *Half-moon* a
room in the tavern   28 *prithee* pray thee (please)   29 *puny* novice, subordi-
nate   32 *precedent* an example, something worth following

Enter [Francis, a] Drawer.

36 FRANCIS Anon, anon, sir. – Look down into the Pomgarnet, Ralph.

PRINCE Come hither, Francis.

FRANCIS My lord?

40 PRINCE How long hast thou to serve, Francis?

FRANCIS Forsooth, five years, and as much as to –

POINS *[Within]* Francis!

FRANCIS Anon, anon, sir.

44 PRINCE Five year! by'r Lady, a long lease for the clinking
of pewter. But, Francis, darest thou be so valiant as to
46 play the coward with thy indenture and show it a fair
pair of heels and run from it?

48 FRANCIS O Lord, sir, I'll be sworn upon all the books in
England I could find in my heart –

50 POINS *[Within]* Francis!

FRANCIS Anon, sir.

PRINCE How old art thou, Francis?

53 FRANCIS Let me see: about Michaelmas next I shall be –

POINS *[Within]* Francis!

55 FRANCIS Anon, sir. Pray stay a little, my lord.

PRINCE Nay, but hark you, Francis. For the sugar thou
gavest me – 'twas a pennyworth, was't not?

FRANCIS O Lord! I would it had been two!

PRINCE I will give thee for it a thousand pound. Ask me
60 when thou wilt, and thou shalt have it.

POINS *[Within]* Francis!

FRANCIS Anon, anon.

PRINCE Anon, Francis? No, Francis; but tomorrow,
Francis; or, Francis, a Thursday; or indeed, Francis,
when thou wilt. But, Francis –

FRANCIS My lord?

36–37 *Pomgarnet* Pomegranate, a room in the tavern   40 *serve* i.e., on his
apprenticeship contract   44 *by'r Lady* by our Lady   46 *indenture* contract
48 *books* Bibles   53 *Michaelmas* September 29   55 *stay a little* wait a moment

PRINCE Wilt thou rob this leathern-jerkin, crystal-button, 67
not-pated, agate-ring, puke-stocking, caddis-garter, 68
smooth-tongue, Spanish-pouch –

FRANCIS O Lord, sir, who do you mean? 70

PRINCE Why then, your brown bastard is your only 71
drink; for look you, Francis, your white canvas doublet 72
will sully. In Barbary, sir, it cannot come to so much. 73

FRANCIS What, sir?

POINS *[Within]* Francis!

PRINCE Away, you rogue! Dost thou not hear them call?
Here they both call him. The Drawer stands amazed,
not knowing which way to go.
Enter Vintner.

VINTNER What, stand'st thou still, and hear'st such a
calling? Look to the guests within. *[Exit Francis.]* My
lord, old Sir John, with half-a-dozen more, are at the
door. Shall I let them in? 80

PRINCE Let them alone awhile, and then open the door.
[Exit Vintner.] Poins!

POINS *[Within]* Anon, anon, sir.
Enter Poins.

PRINCE Sirrah, Falstaff and the rest of the thieves are at
the door. Shall we be merry?

POINS As merry as crickets, my lad. But hark ye; what
cunning match have you made with this jest of the 87
drawer? Come, what's the issue? 88

PRINCE I am now of all humors that have showed them- 89
selves humors since the old days of goodman Adam to 90
the pupil age of this present twelve o'clock at midnight. 91

---

67 *rob* i.e., by running away; *leathern-jerkin* close-fitting sleeveless leather
jacket 68–69 *not-pated . . . pouch* crop-haired, seal-ring-wearing, woolen-
stockinged, worsted-gartered, smooth-talking, Spanish-leather-pouch-
wearing 71 *brown bastard* sweet Spanish wine 72–73 *your . . . sully* you
might as well remain a waiter 73 *it* sugar, imported from Barbary 87 *cunning match* sly game 88 *issue* outcome, punch line 89 *of all humors* in any
moods 90–91 *since . . . midnight* since the days of farmer Adam to now
(i.e., the whole history of the world) 91 *pupil age* i.e., most recent, youngest

[Enter Francis.]
What's o'clock, Francis?

FRANCIS   Anon, anon, sir.   *[Exit.]*

PRINCE   That ever this fellow should have fewer words
than a parrot, and yet the son of a woman! His industry
96   is upstairs and downstairs, his eloquence the parcel of a
reckoning. I am not yet of Percy's mind, the Hotspur of
98   the North; he that kills me some six or seven dozen of
Scots at a breakfast, washes his hands, and says to his
100   wife, "Fie upon this quiet life! I want work." "O my
sweet Harry," says she, "how many hast thou killed
102   today?" "Give my roan horse a drench," says he, and
answers "Some fourteen," an hour after, "a trifle, a trifle." I prithee call in Falstaff. I'll play Percy, and that
105   damned brawn shall play Dame Mortimer his wife.
106   "Rivo!" says the drunkard. Call in ribs, call in tallow.

*Enter Falstaff [, Gadshill, Bardolph, and Peto; Francis
follows with wine].*

POINS   Welcome, Jack. Where hast thou been?

FALSTAFF   A plague of all cowards, I say, and a vengeance
too! Marry and amen! Give me a cup of sack, boy. Ere I
110   lead this life long, I'll sew netherstocks, and mend them
111   and foot them too. A plague of all cowards! Give me a
112   cup of sack, rogue. Is there no virtue extant?

He drinketh.

113   PRINCE   Didst thou never see Titan kiss a dish of but-
114   ter (pitiful-hearted Titan!) that melted at the sweet
115   tale of the sun's? If thou didst, then behold that compound.

117   FALSTAFF   You rogue, here's lime in this sack too! There is
nothing but roguery to be found in villainous man. Yet

96–97 *parcel of a reckoning* items of a bill   **98** *kills me* kills   **102** *drench*
drink   **105** *brawn* fat boar   **106** *Rivo!* (drinking cry, of uncertain meaning);
ribs rib roast; *tallow* grease   **110** *sew netherstocks* make stockings (a menial
occupation)   **111** *foot* make a new foot for   **112** *extant* still living   **113**
Titan the sun   **114** *that* i.e., the butter   **115–16** *compound* sweating (melt-
ing) lump of butter   **117** *lime* caustic powder (calcium carbonate) added to
wine to make it sparkle

a coward is worse than a cup of sack with lime in it – a
villainous coward! Go thy ways, old Jack, die when   *120*
thou wilt; if manhood, good manhood, be not forgot
upon the face of the earth, then am I a shotten herring.   *122*
There lives not three good men unhanged in England;
and one of them is fat, and grows old. God help the
while! A bad world, I say. I would I were a weaver; I   *125*
could sing psalms or anything. A plague of all cowards,
I say still!

PRINCE   How now, woolsack? What mutter you?

FALSTAFF   A king's son! If I do not beat thee out of thy
kingdom with a dagger of lath and drive all thy subjects   *130*
afore thee like a flock of wild geese, I'll never wear hair
on my face more. You Prince of Wales?

PRINCE   Why, you whoreson round man, what's the
matter?

FALSTAFF   Are not you a coward? Answer me to that –
and Poins there?

POINS   Zounds, ye fat paunch, an ye call me coward, by   *137*
the Lord, I'll stab thee.

FALSTAFF   I call thee coward? I'll see thee damned ere I
call thee coward, but I would give a thousand pound I   *140*
could run as fast as thou canst. You are straight enough
in the shoulders; you care not who sees your back. Call
you that backing of your friends? A plague upon such
backing! Give me them that will face me. Give me a
cup of sack. I am a rogue if I drunk today.

PRINCE   O villain! thy lips are scarce wiped since thou
drunk'st last.

FALSTAFF   All is one for that. *(He drinketh.)* A plague of   *148*
all cowards, still say I.

PRINCE   What's the matter?   *150*

---

122 *shotten herring* herring that has shed its eggs and is thus thin, deflated
125 *while* these times; *weaver* (weavers were often immigrants, known for
Protestant devotion; with some allusion to Falstaff's historical prototype?)
130 *lath* thin strip of wood (the weapon of the Vice figure in a morality play)
137 *an* if   148 *All is one* no matter

FALSTAFF   What's the matter? There be four of us here
have ta'en a thousand pound this day morning.

PRINCE   Where is it, Jack? where is it?

FALSTAFF   Where is it? Taken from us it is. A hundred
upon poor four of us!

PRINCE   What, a hundred, man?

157   FALSTAFF   I am a rogue if I were not at half-sword with a
dozen of them two hours together. I have scaped by
159   miracle. I am eight times thrust through the doublet,
160   four through the hose; my buckler cut through and
161   through; my sword hacked like a handsaw – ecce
162   signum! I never dealt better since I was a man. All
would not do. A plague of all cowards! Let them speak.
If they speak more or less than truth, they are villains
and the sons of darkness.

PRINCE   Speak, sirs. How was it?

GADSHILL   We four set upon some dozen –

FALSTAFF   Sixteen at least, my lord.

GADSHILL   And bound them.

170   PETO   No, no, they were not bound.

FALSTAFF   You rogue, they were bound, every man of
172   them, or I am a Jew else – an Ebrew Jew.

GADSHILL   As we were sharing, some six or seven fresh
men set upon us –

FALSTAFF   And unbound the rest, and then come in the
176   other.

PRINCE   What, fought you with them all?

FALSTAFF   All? I know not what you call all, but if I
fought not with fifty of them, I am a bunch of radish! If
180   there were not two or three and fifty upon poor old
Jack, then am I no two-legged creature.

PRINCE   Pray God you have not murdered some of them.

---

157 *at half-sword* fighting at close quarters   159 *doublet* a jacketlike garment
160 *hose* close-fitting pants; *buckler* shield   161–62 *ecce signum* behold the
proof (a term from the liturgy)   162 *dealt* i.e., blows   162–63 *All . . . do*
but to no avail   172 *Ebrew* Hebrew (a [Christian] term for the faithless)
176 *other* others

FALSTAFF   Nay, that's past praying for. I have peppered   183
two of them. Two I am sure I have paid, two rogues in
buckram suits. I tell thee what, Hal – if I tell thee a lie,
spit in my face, call me horse. Thou knowest my old   186
ward. Here I lay, and thus I bore my point. Four rogues   187
in buckram let drive at me.   188

PRINCE   What, four? Thou saidst but two even now.

FALSTAFF   Four, Hal. I told thee four.   190

POINS   Ay, ay, he said four.

FALSTAFF   These four came all afront and mainly thrust   192
at me. I made me no more ado but took all their seven   193
points in my target, thus.   194

PRINCE   Seven? Why, there were but four even now.

FALSTAFF   In buckram?

POINS   Ay, four, in buckram suits.

FALSTAFF   Seven, by these hilts, or I am a villain else.

PRINCE   *[Aside to Poins]* Prithee let him alone. We shall
have more anon.

FALSTAFF   Dost thou hear me, Hal?   200

PRINCE   Ay, and mark thee too, Jack.   201

FALSTAFF   Do so, for it is worth the list'ning to. These
nine in buckram that I told thee of –

PRINCE   So, two more already.

FALSTAFF   Their points being broken –   205

POINS   Down fell their hose.

FALSTAFF   Began to give me ground; but I followed me   207
close, came in, foot and hand, and with a thought   208
seven of the eleven I paid.   209

PRINCE   O monstrous! Eleven buckram men grown out   210
of two!

---

183 *peppered* killed, made it hot for   186 *horse* term of contempt   187
ward defensive stance; *lay* stood; *point* sword point   188 *let drive* came at
192 *afront* abreast   193 *made me* i.e., made   194 *target* shield   201 *mark*
(1) pay attention to, (2) keep count   205 *points* (1) sword points, (2) laces
that hold up hose to doublet   207 *followed me* followed   208 *came in* advanced; *with a thought* as quick as a thought   209 *paid* beat

FALSTAFF   But, as the devil would have it, three misbe-
213   gotten knaves in Kendal green came at my back and let
drive at me; for it was so dark, Hal, that thou couldst
not see thy hand.

PRINCE   These lies are like their father that begets them –
217   gross as a mountain, open, palpable. Why, thou clay-
218   brained guts, thou knotty-pated fool, thou whoreson
219   obscene greasy tallow-keech –

220   FALSTAFF   What, art thou mad? art thou mad? Is not the
truth the truth?

PRINCE   Why, how couldst thou know these men in
Kendal green when it was so dark thou couldst not see
thy hand? Come, tell us your reason. What sayest thou
to this?

POINS   Come, your reason, Jack, your reason.

FALSTAFF   What, upon compulsion? Zounds, an I were at
228   the strappado or all the racks in the world, I would not
tell you on compulsion. Give you a reason on compul-
230   sion? If reasons were as plentiful as blackberries, I
would give no man a reason upon compulsion, I.

232   PRINCE   I'll be no longer guilty of this sin; this sanguine
coward, this bed-presser, this horseback-breaker, this
huge hill of flesh –

FALSTAFF   'Sblood, you starveling, you eel-skin, you
236   dried neat's-tongue, you bull's pizzle, you stockfish – O
237   for breath to utter what is like thee! – you tailor's yard,
238   you sheath, you bowcase, you vile standing tuck!

PRINCE   Well, breathe awhile, and then to it again; and
240   when thou hast tired thyself in base comparisons, hear
me speak but this.

POINS   Mark, Jack.

---

213 *Kendal* a famous textile town   217 *palpable* easily perceptible   218
knotty-pated thickheaded   219 *tallow-keech* lump of tallow   228 *strappado* a
torture in which the victim was hoisted by a rope and let drop its length;
racks a torture instrument upon which the body is stretched   230 *reasons*
(pun on "raisins")   232 *sanguine* ruddy, confident   236 *neat's* ox's; *pizzle*
penis; *stockfish* dried cod   237 *yard* yardstick   238 *standing tuck* rigid rapier
(which was supposed to be flexible)

PRINCE   We two saw you four set on four, and bound
them and were masters of their wealth. Mark now how
a plain tale shall put you down. Then did we two set on
you four and, with a word, outfaced you from your   246
prize, and have it; yea, and can show it you here in the
house. And, Falstaff, you carried your guts away as
nimbly, with as quick dexterity, and roared for mercy,
and still run and roared, as ever I heard bullcalf. What a   250
slave art thou to hack thy sword as thou hast done, and
then say it was in fight! What trick, what device, what
starting hole canst thou now find out to hide thee from   253
this open and apparent shame?

POINS   Come, let's hear, Jack. What trick hast thou now?

FALSTAFF   By the Lord, I knew ye as well as he that made
ye. Why, hear you, my masters. Was it for me to kill the
heir apparent? Should I turn upon the true prince?   258
Why, thou knowest I am as valiant as Hercules, but be-   259
ware instinct. The lion will not touch the true prince.   260
Instinct is a great matter. I was now a coward on instinct. I shall think the better of myself, and thee, during my life – I for a valiant lion, and thou for a true
prince. But, by the Lord, lads, I am glad you have the
money. Hostess, clap to the doors. Watch tonight, pray   265
tomorrow. Gallants, lads, boys, hearts of gold, all the titles of good fellowship come to you! What, shall we be
merry? Shall we have a play extempore?   268

PRINCE   Content – and the argument shall be thy run-   269
ning away.   270

FALSTAFF   Ah, no more of that, Hal, an thou lovest me!
   Enter Hostess.

HOSTESS   O Jesu, my lord the prince!

PRINCE   How now, my lady the hostess? What say'st thou
to me?

---

246 *with a word* in short; *outfaced* frightened   253 *starting hole* subterfuge,
(literally) refuge for hunted animals   258 *heir apparent* next in line to the
throne   259 *Hercules* legendary strong man   259–60 *beware* watch out for
265–66 *Watch . . . tomorrow* see Matthew 26:41   268 *play extempore* an im-
provised play   269 *argument* plot

HOSTESS   Marry, my lord, there is a noble man of the
court at door would speak with you. He says he comes
from your father.

278 PRINCE   Give him as much as will make him a royal man,
and send him back again to my mother.

280 FALSTAFF   What manner of man is he?

HOSTESS   An old man.

282 FALSTAFF   What doth gravity out of his bed at midnight?
Shall I give him his answer?

PRINCE   Prithee do, Jack.

FALSTAFF   Faith, and I'll send him packing.   *Exit*.

286 PRINCE   Now, sirs. By'r Lady, you fought fair; so did you,
Peto; so did you, Bardolph. You are lions too, you ran
away upon instinct, you will not touch the true prince;
no – fie!

290 BARDOLPH   Faith, I ran when I saw others run.

PRINCE   Tell me now in earnest, how came Falstaff's
sword so hacked?

PETO   Why, he hacked it with his dagger, and said he
294 would swear truth out of England but he would make
you believe it was done in fight, and persuaded us to do
the like.

BARDOLPH   Yea, and to tickle our noses with speargrass
to make them bleed, and then to beslubber our garments with it and swear it was the blood of true men. I
300 did that I did not this seven year before – I blushed to
301 hear his monstrous devices.

PRINCE   O villain! thou stolest a cup of sack eighteen
303 years ago and wert taken with the manner, and ever
304 since thou hast blushed extempore. Thou hadst fire and
sword on thy side, and yet thou ran'st away. What instinct hadst thou for it?

---

278 *a royal man* a royal was a coin worth 10 shillings; a noble, 6 shillings
8 pence 282 *gravity* age, wisdom 286 *fair* well 294 *but . . . would* if he
didn't 300 *that* what 301 *devices* tricks 303 *taken . . . manner* caught
with the goods 304 *extempore* without preparation; *fire* i.e., Bardolph's
nose, red from drinking

BARDOLPH   My lord, do you see these meteors? Do you
behold these exhalations?   308

PRINCE   I do.

BARDOLPH   What think you they portend?   310

PRINCE   Hot livers and cold purses.   311

BARDOLPH   Choler, my lord, if rightly taken.   312

PRINCE   No, if rightly taken, halter.   313

   Enter Falstaff.

Here comes lean Jack; here comes barebone. How now,
my sweet creature of bombast? How long is't ago, Jack,   315
since thou sawest thine own knee?

FALSTAFF   My own knee? When I was about thy years,
Hal, I was not an eagle's talent in the waist; I could   318
have crept into any alderman's thumb ring. A plague of
sighing and grief! It blows a man up like a bladder.   320
There's villainous news abroad. Here was Sir John
Bracy from your father. You must to the court in the
morning. That same mad fellow of the north, Percy,
and he of Wales that gave Amamon the bastinado, and   324
made Lucifer cuckold, and swore the devil his true   325
liegeman upon the cross of a Welsh hook – what a   326
plague call you him?

POINS   Owen Glendower.

FALSTAFF   Owen, Owen – the same; and his son-in-law
Mortimer, and old Northumberland, and that sprightly   330
Scot of Scots, Douglas, that runs a-horseback up a hill
perpendicular –

PRINCE   He that rides at high speed and with his pistol
kills a sparrow flying.

---

308 *exhalations* meteors (i.e., red spots on Bardolph's face)   311 *Hot livers
and cold purses* i.e., drunkenness and poverty   312 *Choler* anger, aggression;
taken understood   313 *halter* i.e., collar (a play on choler), or hangman's
noose   315 *bombast* (1) cotton padding, (2) outrageous speech   318 *talent*
talon   324 *Amamon* name of a demon; *bastinado* beating on soles of the feet
325 *made Lucifer cuckold* gave the devil his horns (a sign of cuckoldry)   326
liegeman sworn subject; *Welsh hook* a curved pike lacking the cross handle of
a sword upon which oaths were usually sworn

335 FALSTAFF You have hit it.

PRINCE So did he never the sparrow.

337 FALSTAFF Well, that rascal hath good metal in him; he will not run.

PRINCE Why, what a rascal art thou then, to praise him
340 so for running!

FALSTAFF A-horseback, ye cuckoo! but afoot he will not budge a foot.

PRINCE Yes, Jack, upon instinct.

FALSTAFF I grant ye, upon instinct. Well, he is there too,
345 and one Mordake, and a thousand bluecaps more. Worcester is stol'n away tonight; thy father's beard is turned white with the news; you may buy land now as cheap as stinking mack'rel.

349 PRINCE Why then, it is like, if there come a hot June,
350 and this civil buffeting hold, we shall buy maidenheads
351 as they buy hobnails, by the hundreds.

FALSTAFF By the mass, lad, thou sayest true; it is like we
353 shall have good trading that way. But tell me, Hal, art not thou horrible afeard? Thou being heir apparent, could the world pick thee out three such enemies again as that fiend Douglas, that spirit Percy, and that devil Glendower? Art thou not horribly afraid? Doth not thy
358 blood thrill at it?

PRINCE Not a whit, i' faith. I lack some of thy instinct.

360 FALSTAFF Well, thou wilt be horribly chid tomorrow when thou comest to thy father. If thou love me, practice an answer.

363 PRINCE Do thou stand for my father and examine me upon the particulars of my life.

365 FALSTAFF Shall I? Content. This chair shall be my state, this dagger my scepter, and this cushion my crown.

---

335 *hit it* described it 337 *metal* mettle, temperament, courage 345 *Mordake* i.e., Murdoch; *bluecaps* Scottish soldiers 349 *like* likely 350 *buffeting* war, fighting; *maidenheads* hymens, or virginities, a spoil of war 351 *hobnails* a short broad-headed nail sold in bulk 353 *good . . . way* i.e., lots of women 358 *thrill* run cold 360 *chid* reprimanded 363 *stand for* take the place of 365 *state* throne

PRINCE   Thy state is taken for a joined stool, thy golden   367
scepter for a leaden dagger, and thy precious rich crown   368
for a pitiful bald crown.

FALSTAFF   Well, an the fire of grace be not quite out of   370
thee, now shalt thou be moved. Give me a cup of sack
to make my eyes look red, that it may be thought I have
wept; for I must speak in passion, and I will do it in
King Cambyses' vein.   374

PRINCE   Well, here is my leg.   375

FALSTAFF   And here is my speech. Stand aside, nobility.

HOSTESS   O Jesu, this is excellent sport, i' faith!

FALSTAFF
Weep not, sweet queen, for trickling tears are vain.

HOSTESS   O, the Father, how he holds his countenance!   379

FALSTAFF
For God's sake, lords, convey my tristful queen!   380
For tears do stop the floodgates of her eyes.   381

HOSTESS   O Jesu, he doth it as like one of these harlotry   382
players as ever I see!

FALSTAFF   Peace, good pintpot. Peace, good tickle-   384
brain. – Harry, I do not only marvel where thou spend-
est thy time, but also how thou art accompanied. For
though the camomile, the more it is trodden on, the   387
faster it grows, yet youth, the more it is wasted, the
sooner it wears. That thou art my son I have partly thy
mother's word, partly my own opinion, but chiefly a   390
villainous trick of thine eye and a foolish hanging of   391
thy nether lip that doth warrant me. If then thou be   392
son to me, here lies the point: why, being son to me, art
thou so pointed at? Shall the blessed sun of heaven

---

367 *taken for* understood to be; *joined stool* a stool made of fitted parts (to
"take someone for a joint stool" is an apology for overlooking them)   368
crown (1) head, (2) coin   370 *an* if   374 *King Cambyses' vein* a ranting, an
outdated theatrical style (from Thomas Preston's 1569 play)   375 *leg* bow
379 *holds his countenance* keeps a straight face   380 *convey* escort away; *tristful* sad   381 *stop* fill, overflow   382 *harlotry* scurvy, vagabond   384–85
pintpot, ticklebrain (nicknames based on the hostess's occupation)   387
camomile an herb   391 *trick* trait   392 *warrant* assure

395   prove a micher and eat blackberries? A question not to
        be asked. Shall the son of England prove a thief and
397   take purses? A question to be asked. There is a thing,
        Harry, which thou hast often heard of, and it is known
399   to many in our land by the name of pitch. This pitch,
400   as ancient writers do report, doth defile; so doth the
        company thou keepest. For, Harry, now I do not speak
        to thee in drink, but in tears; not in pleasure, but in
        passion; not in words only, but in woes also. And yet
        there is a virtuous man whom I have often noted in thy
        company, but I know not his name.

406 PRINCE   What manner of man, an it like your majesty?

407 FALSTAFF   A goodly portly man, i' faith, and a corpulent;
408   of a cheerful look, a pleasing eye, and a most noble car-
        riage; and, as I think, his age some fifty, or, by'r Lady,
410   inclining to threescore; and now I remember me, his
411   name is Falstaff. If that man should be lewdly given, he
        deceiveth me; for, Harry, I see virtue in his looks. If
413   then the tree may be known by the fruit, as the fruit by
414   the tree, then, peremptorily I speak it, there is virtue in
        that Falstaff. Him keep with, the rest banish. And tell
416   me now, thou naughty varlet, tell me where hast thou
        been this month?

     PRINCE   Dost thou speak like a king? Do thou stand for
        me, and I'll play my father.

420 FALSTAFF   Depose me? If thou dost it half so gravely, so
        majestically, both in word and matter, hang me up by
422   the heels for a rabbit-sucker or a poulter's hare.

---

395 *micher* truant   **397** *purses* (perhaps with a pun on "Percies")   **399** *pitch*
a tar by-product (a reference to a proverb from Ecclesiastes 13:1)   **406** *an it*
like if it please   **407** *goodly* (1) handsome, (2) sizable; *portly* (1) large, (2)
dignified; *corpulent* fat   **408–9** *carriage* bearing, posture   **410** *threescore*
sixty   **411** *lewdly given* disposed to wickedness   **413–14** see Matthew 12:33
414 *peremptorily* decisively   **416** *varlet* rascal   **420** *Depose me?* (Falstaff jokes
that Hal will force him from the throne – much as Henry IV did Richard II)
422 *rabbit-sucker* unweaned rabbit; *poulter's* poulterer's (vendor of dead
chickens and rabbits)

PRINCE   Well, here I am set.

FALSTAFF   And here I stand. Judge, my masters.

PRINCE   Now, Harry, whence come you?

FALSTAFF   My noble lord, from Eastcheap.

PRINCE   The complaints I hear of thee are grievous.

FALSTAFF   'Sblood, my lord, they are false! Nay, I'll tickle   428
ye for a young prince, i' faith.

PRINCE   Swearest thou, ungracious boy? Henceforth   *430*
ne'er look on me. Thou art violently carried away from
grace. There is a devil haunts thee in the likeness of   432
an old fat man; a tun of man is thy companion. Why   433
dost thou converse with that trunk of humors, that   434
bolting hutch of beastliness, that swoll'n parcel of   435
dropsies, that huge bombard of sack, that stuffed cloak-   436
bag of guts, that roasted Manningtree ox with the pud-   437
ding in his belly, that reverend Vice, that gray iniquity,   438
that father ruffian, that vanity in years? Wherein is he   439
good, but to taste sack and drink it? wherein neat and   440
cleanly, but to carve a capon and eat it? wherein cun-   441
ning, but in craft? wherein crafty, but in villainy?   442
wherein villainous, but in all things? wherein worthy,
but in nothing?

FALSTAFF   I would your grace would take me with you.   445
Whom means your grace?

PRINCE   That villainous abominable misleader of youth,
Falstaff, that old white-bearded Satan.

FALSTAFF   My lord, the man I know.

PRINCE   I know thou dost.   *450*

---

428 *'Sblood* by God's blood   **428–29** *tickle ye for* amuse you in the role of
432 *grace* (1) royalty, (2) divine grace   **433** *tun* (1) ton, (2) barrel   **434** *converse* talk with, associate with; *humors* body fluids   **435** *bolting hutch* large
flour bin   **436** *dropsies* watery swellings; *bombard* leather drinking vessel
437 *Manningtree ox* notoriously large ox roasted whole in Essex, a town famous for fairs   **437–38** *pudding in his belly* stuffing in intestines   **438** *reverend Vice . . . iniquity* name for chief tempter in morality plays   **439** *vanity*
worldly person   **441–42** *cunning* skillful   **442** *craft* trickery   **445** *take . . .
you* make yourself clear

FALSTAFF   But to say I know more harm in him than in
myself were to say more than I know. That he is old
(the more the pity), his white hairs do witness it; but
454   that he is (saving your reverence) a whoremaster, that I
utterly deny. If sack and sugar be a fault, God help the
wicked! If to be old and merry be a sin, then many an
457   old host that I know is damned. If to be fat be to be
458   hated, then Pharaoh's lean kine are to be loved. No, my
good lord: banish Peto, banish Bardolph, banish Poins;
460   but for sweet Jack Falstaff, kind Jack Falstaff, true Jack
Falstaff, valiant Jack Falstaff, and therefore more valiant
being, as he is, old Jack Falstaff, banish not him thy
Harry's company, banish not him thy Harry's company.
Banish plump Jack, and banish all the world!
PRINCE   I do, I will.
    [A knocking heard.]
            [Exeunt Hostess, Francis, and Bardolph.]
    Enter Bardolph, running.
BARDOLPH   O, my lord, my lord! the sheriff with a most
467   monstrous watch is at the door.
FALSTAFF   Out, ye rogue! Play out the play. I have much
to say in the behalf of that Falstaff.
    Enter the Hostess.
470   HOSTESS   O Jesu, my lord, my lord!
471   PRINCE   Heigh, heigh, the devil rides upon a fiddlestick!
What's the matter?
HOSTESS   The sheriff and all the watch are at the door.
They are come to search the house. Shall I let them in?
475   FALSTAFF   Dost thou hear, Hal? Never call a true piece of
gold a counterfeit. Thou art essentially mad without
seeming so.

---

454 *saving your reverence* with my apologies for rough language; *whoremaster*
one who consorts with prostitutes   457 *host* innkeeper   458 *Pharaoh's lean
kine* see Genesis 41:3–4; *kine* cows   467 *watch* constabulary   471 *devil . . .
fiddlestick* here's much ado about nothing   475–77 *Never . . . so* don't call
me, a true fellow, false (i.e., betray me to the watch); you are one of us even
though you don't seem it

PRINCE   And thou a natural coward without instinct.

FALSTAFF   I deny your major. If you will deny the sheriff, 479
so; if not, let him enter. If I become not a cart as well as 480
another man, a plague on my bringing up! I hope I
shall as soon be strangled with a halter as another.

PRINCE   Go hide thee behind the arras. The rest walk up 483
above. Now, my masters, for a true face and good con- 484
science.

FALSTAFF   Both which I have had; but their date is out, 486
and therefore I'll hide me.   *Exit.*

PRINCE   Call in the sheriff.
     [Exeunt. The Prince and Peto remain behind.]
    Enter Sheriff and the Carrier.
Now, master sheriff, what is your will with me?

SHERIFF
First, pardon me, my lord. A hue and cry   490
Hath followed certain men unto this house.

PRINCE
What men?

SHERIFF
One of them is well known, my gracious lord –
A gross fat man.

CARRIER   As fat as butter.

PRINCE
The man, I do assure you, is not here,
For I myself at this time have employed him.
And, sheriff, I will engage my word to thee   497
That I will by tomorrow dinnertime
Send him to answer thee, or any man,
For anything he shall be charged withal;   500
And so let me entreat you leave the house.   501

SHERIFF
I will, my lord. There are two gentlemen

---

479 *major* major premise; *deny the sheriff* refuse admittance to   480 *a cart* a
hangman's cart   483 *arras* wall hanging   484 *true* straight, honest   486
date is out time is past   497 *engage* promise   501 *entreat* beg

Have in this robbery lost three hundred marks.

PRINCE
It may be so. If he have robbed these men,
He shall be answerable; and so farewell.

SHERIFF
Good night, my noble lord.

PRINCE
507   I think it is good morrow, is it not?

SHERIFF
Indeed, my lord, I think it be two o'clock.

Exit [with Carrier].

509   PRINCE   This oily rascal is known as well as Paul's. Go
510   call him forth.

511   PETO   Falstaff! Fast asleep behind the arras, and snorting
like a horse.

PRINCE   Hark how hard he fetches breath. Search his
pockets.
He searcheth his pockets and findeth certain papers.
What hast thou found?

PETO   Nothing but papers, my lord.

PRINCE   Let's see what they be. Read them.

PETO   *[Reads.]*

518   "Item, A capon . . . . ii s. ii d.
Item, Sauce . . . . iiii d.
520   Item, Sack two gallons . . . . v s. viii d.
Item, Anchovies and sack after supper . ii s. vi d.
522   Item, Bread . . . . ob."

PRINCE   O monstrous! but one halfpennyworth of bread
to this intolerable deal of sack! What there is else, keep
525   close; we'll read it at more advantage. There let him
sleep till day. I'll to the court in the morning. We must
all to the wars, and thy place shall be honorable. I'll

---

507 *morrow* tomorrow   509 *Paul's* Saint Paul's Cathedral, at the center of
London   511 *snorting* snoring   518 *Item* . . . a bill for goods; *capon* male
fowl; *ii s. ii d.* two shillings twopence   522 *ob* obulus, a halfpenny   525 *close*
secret, hidden; *at more advantage* at better opportunity

procure this fat rogue a charge of foot, and I know his   528
death will be a march of twelvescore. The money shall   529
be paid back again with advantage. Be with me betimes   530
in the morning, and so good morrow, Peto.

PETO   Good morrow, good my lord.   *Exeunt.*

                          ✳

❧ **III.1** *Enter Hotspur, Worcester, Lord Mortimer, Owen*
     Glendower.

MORTIMER
     These promises are fair, the parties sure,   1
     And our induction full of prosperous hope.   2

HOTSPUR   Lord Mortimer, and cousin Glendower, will
     you sit down? And uncle Worcester. A plague upon it! I
     have forgot the map.

GLENDOWER
     No, here it is. Sit, cousin Percy;
     Sit, good cousin Hotspur, for by that name
     As oft as Lancaster doth speak of you,   8
     His cheek looks pale, and with a rising sigh
     He wisheth you in heaven.   10

HOTSPUR   And you in hell, as oft as he hears Owen Glen-
     dower spoke of.

GLENDOWER
     I cannot blame him. At my nativity   13
     The front of heaven was full of fiery shapes   14
     Of burning cressets, and at my birth   15
     The frame and huge foundation of the earth
     Shaked like a coward.

---

528 *charge of foot* command of a company of foot soldiers   **529** *twelvescore*
i.e., 240 yards   **530** *advantage* interest; *betimes* early
     III.1 Glendower's castle in Wales   **1** *the parties sure* the partners are cer-
tain, promised   **2** *induction* beginning; *prosperous hope* hope of success
8 *Lancaster* the king   **13** *nativity* birth   **14** *front* brow   **15** *cressets* lights
burning in baskets atop poles (i.e., meteors)

HOTSPUR   Why, so it would have done at the same season if your mother's cat had but kittened, though your-
20   self had never been born.

GLENDOWER
I say the earth did shake when I was born.

HOTSPUR
And I say the earth was not of my mind,
If you suppose as fearing you it shook.

GLENDOWER
The heavens were all on fire, the earth did tremble.

HOTSPUR
O, then the earth shook to see the heavens on fire,
And not in fear of your nativity.
Diseasèd nature oftentimes breaks forth
In strange eruptions; oft the teeming earth
29   Is with a kind of colic pinched and vexed
30   By the imprisoning of unruly wind
31   Within her womb, which, for enlargement striving,
32   Shakes the old beldame earth and topples down
Steeples and moss-grown towers. At your birth
34   Our grandam earth, having this distemp'rature,
In passion shook.

GLENDOWER   Cousin, of many men
36   I do not bear these crossings. Give me leave
To tell you once again that at my birth
The front of heaven was full of fiery shapes,
The goats ran from the mountains, and the herds
40   Were strangely clamorous to the frighted fields.
These signs have marked me extraordinary,
42   And all the courses of my life do show
43   I am not in the roll of common men.
44   Where is he living, clipped in with the sea

---

29 *colic* abdominal spasm   31 *enlargement* release, escape   32 *beldame*
grandmother   34 *distemp'rature* ailment   36 *crossings* contradictions   40
clamorous in confused outcry   42 *courses* events   43 *roll* roster, rank   44
clipped in surrounded by

That chides the banks of England, Scotland, Wales,   45
Which calls me pupil or hath read to me?   46
And bring him out that is but woman's son
Can trace me in the tedious ways of art   48
And hold me pace in deep experiments.   49

HOTSPUR   I think there's no man speaks better Welsh. I'll   50
to dinner.

MORTIMER
Peace, cousin Percy; you will make him mad.

GLENDOWER
I can call spirits from the vasty deep.   53

HOTSPUR
Why, so can I, or so can any man;
But will they come when you do call for them?

GLENDOWER   Why, I can teach you, cousin, to command the devil.

HOTSPUR
And I can teach thee, coz, to shame the devil –
By telling truth. Tell truth and shame the devil.
If thou have power to raise him, bring him hither,   60
And I'll be sworn I have power to shame him hence.
O, while you live, tell truth and shame the devil!

MORTIMER
Come, come, no more of this unprofitable chat.

GLENDOWER
Three times hath Henry Bolingbroke made head   64
Against my power; thrice from the banks of Wye   65
And sandy-bottomed Severn have I sent him   66
Bootless home and weather-beaten back.   67

HOTSPUR
Home without boots, and in foul weather too?
How scapes he agues, in the devil's name?   69

---

45 *chides* lashes, rebukes 46 *Which* who; *read to* instructed 48 *trace* follow;
tedious laborious; *art* magic 49 *hold me pace* keep up with me 50 *Welsh*
(derogatory term for boasting and/or nonsensical speech) 53 *vasty deep* lower
world 64 *made head* raised troops 65, 66 *Wye, Severn* rivers that border
Wales 67 *Bootless* without gain 69 *agues* fevers

GLENDOWER

70 Come, here is the map. Shall we divide our right
71 According to our threefold order ta'en?

MORTIMER

72 The archdeacon hath divided it
    Into three limits very equally.
74 England, from Trent and Severn hitherto,
    By south and east is to my part assigned;
    All westward, Wales beyond the Severn shore,
77 And all the fertile land within that bound,
78 To Owen Glendower; and, dear coz, to you
79 The remnant northward lying off from Trent.
80 And our indentures tripartite are drawn,
81 Which being sealèd interchangeably
82 (A business that this night may execute),
    Tomorrow, cousin Percy, you and I
    And my good Lord of Worcester will set forth
    To meet your father and the Scottish power,
    As is appointed us, at Shrewsbury.
87 My father Glendower is not ready yet,
    Nor shall we need his help these fourteen days.
       [To Glendower]
89 Within that space you may have drawn together
90 Your tenants, friends, and neighboring gentlemen.

GLENDOWER

    A shorter time shall send me to you, lords;
92 And in my conduct shall your ladies come,
93 From whom you now must steal and take no leave,
    For there will be a world of water shed
    Upon the parting of your wives and you.

---

70 *right* possession   71 *order ta'en* arrangement   72 *archdeacon* i.e., of Bangor, whose house was the historical location for the meeting of the rebel leaders' deputies   74 *Trent* river dividing England from Scotland (roughly speaking, Mortimer takes England; Hotspur, Scotland; and Glendower, Wales)   77 *bound* boundary   78 *coz* i.e., Hotspur   79 *lying off* beyond   80 *indentures . . . drawn* documents are drawn up in triplicate   81 *Which being* which having been   82 *may execute* may accomplish   87 *father* i.e., father-in-law   89 *may* will   92 *conduct* safekeeping   93 *steal* steal away

HOTSPUR
Methinks my moiety, north from Burton here,   96
In quantity equals not one of yours.
See how this river comes me cranking in   98
And cuts me from the best of all my land
A huge half-moon, a monstrous cantle out.   100
I'll have the current in this place dammed up,
And here the smug and silver Trent shall run   102
In a new channel fair and evenly.
It shall not wind with such a deep indent
To rob me of so rich a bottom here.   105

GLENDOWER
Not wind? It shall, it must! You see it doth.

MORTIMER
Yea, but
Mark how he bears his course, and runs me up   108
With like advantage on the other side,
Gelding the opposèd continent as much   110
As on the other side it takes from you.

WORCESTER
Yea, but a little charge will trench him here   112
And on this north side win this cape of land;   113
And then he runs straight and even.

HOTSPUR
I'll have it so. A little charge will do it.

GLENDOWER
I will not have it altered.

HOTSPUR   Will not you?

GLENDOWER
No, nor you shall not.

HOTSPUR   Who shall say me nay?

GLENDOWER
Why, that will I.

----

96 *moiety* share   98 *comes . . . in* comes bending in   100 *cantle* piece   102
smug smooth   105 *bottom* valley   108 *he* i.e., the Trent; *runs me* runs   110
Gelding . . . continent cutting off the land that contains it on the opposite
side   112 *charge* expenditure; *trench* dig a new channel   113 *cape* peninsula

HOTSPUR

Let me not understand you then; speak it in Welsh.

GLENDOWER

120 I can speak English, lord, as well as you;
For I was trained up in the English court,
122 Where, being but young, I framèd to the harp
123 Many an English ditty lovely well,
124 And gave the tongue a helpful ornament –
A virtue that was never seen in you.

HOTSPUR

Marry, and I am glad of it with all my heart!
I had rather be a kitten and cry mew
128 Than one of these same meter ballet-mongers.
129 I had rather hear a brazen canstick turned
130 Or a dry wheel grate on the axletree,
131 And that would set my teeth nothing on edge,
Nothing so much as mincing poetry.
133 'Tis like the forced gait of a shuffling nag.

GLENDOWER

Come, you shall have Trent turned.

HOTSPUR

I do not care. I'll give thrice so much land
To any well-deserving friend;
But in the way of bargain, mark ye me,
138 I'll cavil on the ninth part of a hair.
Are the indentures drawn? Shall we be gone?

GLENDOWER

140 The moon shines fair; you may away by night.
141 I'll haste the writer, and withal
142 Break with your wives of your departure hence.

---

122 *framèd . . . harp* set to the accompaniment of harp music 123 *ditty* song 124 *gave . . . ornament* (1) gave words a decoration of music, (2) gave a musicality to words 128 *meter ballet-mongers* metrical (and hence unartful) ballad makers 129 *brazen canstick turned* brass candlestick turned on a lathe 130 *dry* lacking grease; *axletree* axle 131 *set . . . edge* not set my teeth on edge 133 *shuffling* fettered 138 *cavil . . . hair* argue the smallest detail 141 *haste* hurry; *withal* also 142 *Break with* inform

I am afraid my daughter will run mad,
So much she doteth on her Mortimer.   *Exit.*

MORTIMER

Fie, cousin Percy! how you cross my father!

HOTSPUR

I cannot choose. Sometime he angers me   146
With telling me of the moldwarp and the ant,   147
Of the dreamer Merlin and his prophecies,   148
And of a dragon and a finless fish,
A clip-winged griffin and a molten raven,   150
A couching lion and a ramping cat,   151
And such a deal of skimble-skamble stuff   152
As puts me from my faith. I tell you what –   153
He held me last night at least nine hours
In reckoning up the several devils' names   155
That were his lackeys. I cried "hum," and "well, go to!" 156
But marked him not a word. O, he is as tedious   157
As a tired horse, a railing wife;   158
Worse than a smoky house. I had rather live
With cheese and garlic in a windmill far   *160*
Than feed on cates and have him talk to me   161
In any summer house in Christendom.

MORTIMER

In faith, he is a worthy gentleman,
Exceedingly well read, and profited   164
In strange concealments, valiant as a lion,   165
And wondrous affable, and as bountiful
As mines of India. Shall I tell you, cousin?
He holds your temper in a high respect

---

146 *choose* help it   147 *moldwarp* mole   148 *Merlin* mythical British
(Celtic) magician and seer of the court of King Arthur   150 *griffin* a fabu-
lous beast, half lion, half eagle; *molten* having molted, featherless   151
couching crouching (heraldic term); *ramping* rampant, rearing on hind legs
152 *skimble-skamble* nonsensical, foolish   153 *faith* (1) Christian faith, (2)
good faith toward him; patience   155 *several* various   156 *lackeys* servants;
go to you don't say   157 *marked* paid attention to   158 *railing* ranting   161
cates delicacies   164 *profited* proficient   165 *concealments* secrets

169 And curbs himself even of his natural scope
170 When you come 'cross his humor. Faith, he does.
     I warrant you that man is not alive
     Might so have tempted him as you have done
     Without the taste of danger and reproof.
174 But do not use it oft, let me entreat you.

WORCESTER
175 In faith, my lord, you are too willful-blame,
     And since your coming hither have done enough
177 To put him quite besides his patience.
     You must needs learn, lord, to amend this fault.
179 Though sometimes it show greatness, courage, blood –
180 And that's the dearest grace it renders you –
181 Yet oftentimes it doth present harsh rage,
182 Defect of manners, want of government,
183 Pride, haughtiness, opinion, and disdain;
     The least of which haunting a nobleman
     Loseth men's hearts, and leaves behind a stain
186 Upon the beauty of all parts besides,
187 Beguiling them of commendation.

HOTSPUR
188 Well, I am schooled. Good manners be your speed!
     Here come our wives, and let us take our leave.
          Enter Glendower with the Ladies.

MORTIMER
190 This is the deadly spite that angers me –
     My wife can speak no English, I no Welsh.

GLENDOWER
     My daughter weeps; she will not part with you;
     She'll be a soldier too, she'll to the wars.

---

169 *curbs . . . scope* checks himself from his usual range of responses **170**
come . . . humor contradict his mood, temper **174** *use it* do; *entreat* beg
175 *willful-blame* blameworthy for willfulness **177** *besides* out of **179**
blood spirit, nobility **181** *present* represent **182** *government* self-control
183 *opinion* arrogance **186** *all parts besides* all other parts **187** *Beguiling*
robbing; *commendation* praise **188** *schooled* reprimanded; *be your speed* give
you luck **190** *spite* vexation

MORTIMER

Good father, tell her that she and my aunt Percy   194
Shall follow in your conducts speedily.
Glendower speaks to her in Welsh, and she answers
him in the same.

GLENDOWER

She is desperate here. A peevish self-willed harlotry,   196
One that no persuasion can do good upon.
The Lady speaks in Welsh.

MORTIMER

I understand thy looks. That pretty Welsh
Which thou pourest down from these swelling heavens   199
I am too perfect in; and, but for shame,   200
In such a parley should I answer thee.   201
The Lady again in Welsh.
I understand thy kisses, and thou mine,
And that's a feeling disputation.   203
But I will never be a truant, love,   204
Till I have learnt thy language; for thy tongue
Makes Welsh as sweet as ditties highly penned,   206
Sung by a fair queen in a summer's bow'r,
With ravishing division, to her lute.   208

GLENDOWER

Nay, if you melt, then will she run mad.
The Lady speaks again in Welsh.

MORTIMER

O, I am ignorance itself in this!   *210*

GLENDOWER

She bids you on the wanton rushes lay you down   211
And rest your gentle head upon her lap,

---

194 *aunt* (to Edmund Mortimer, but sister-in-law to Glendower's son-in-
law)   **196** *here* on this score; *self-willed harlotry* willful wench   **199** *swelling*
heavens tearful eyes   **200** *perfect* skilled   **201** *such a parley* a similar tongue
(i.e., weeping)   **203** *feeling disputation* emotional conversation, exchange
204 *truant* unfaithful man   **206** *highly penned* eloquently, nobly composed
208 *division* musical variation   **211** *wanton* luxurious; *rushes* reeds used for
floor covering

And she will sing the song that pleaseth you
214   And on your eyelids crown the god of sleep,
215   Charming your blood with pleasing heaviness,
Making such difference 'twixt wake and sleep
As is the difference betwixt day and night
218   The hour before the heavenly-harnessed team
Begins his golden progress in the east.

MORTIMER
220   With all my heart I'll sit and hear her sing.
221   By that time will our book, I think, be drawn.

GLENDOWER
Do so, and those musicians that shall play to you
Hang in the air a thousand leagues from hence,
And straight they shall be here. Sit, and attend.

225   HOTSPUR   Come, Kate, thou art perfect in lying down.
Come, quick, quick, that I may lay my head in thy lap.

LADY PERCY   Go, ye giddy goose.
   The music plays.

HOTSPUR
Now I perceive the devil understands Welsh.
229   And 'tis no marvel he is so humorous,
230   By'r Lady, he is a good musician.

LADY PERCY   Then should you be nothing but musical,
for you are altogether governed by humors. Lie still, ye
thief, and hear the lady sing in Welsh.

234   HOTSPUR   I had rather hear Lady, my brach, howl in
235   Irish.

LADY PERCY   Wouldst thou have thy head broken?
HOTSPUR   No.
LADY PERCY   Then be still.
239   HOTSPUR   Neither! 'Tis a woman's fault.
240   LADY PERCY   Now God help thee!
HOTSPUR   To the Welsh lady's bed.

---

214 *crown* give dominion to 215 *blood* mood; *heaviness* sleepiness **218**
team (of horses drawing the chariot of the sun) **221** *book* documents **225**
perfect skilled; *lying down* sexual congress **229** *humorous* full of moods,
whims **234** *brach* female hound **235** *Irish* (considered an even more con-
temptible language than Welsh) **239** *Neither* not that either

LADY PERCY   What's that?

HOTSPUR   Peace! she sings.

Here the Lady sings a Welsh song.

Come, Kate, I'll have your song too.

LADY PERCY   Not mine, in good sooth.   245

HOTSPUR   Not yours, in good sooth? Heart! you swear   246
like a comfit-maker's wife. "Not you, in good sooth!"   247
and "as true as I live!" and "as God shall mend me!" and
"as sure as day!"

And givest such sarcenet surety for thy oaths   250
As if thou never walk'st further than Finsbury.   251
Swear me, Kate, like a lady as thou art,   252
A good mouth-filling oath, and leave "in sooth"
And such protest of pepper gingerbread   254
To velvet guards and Sunday citizens.   255
Come, sing.

LADY PERCY   I will not sing.

HOTSPUR   'Tis the next way to turn tailor or be red-   258
breast teacher. An the indentures be drawn, I'll away
within these two hours; and so come in when ye will.   260

Exit.

GLENDOWER

Come, come, Lord Mortimer. You are as slow
As hot Lord Percy is on fire to go.
By this our book is drawn; we'll but seal,   263
And then to horse immediately.

MORTIMER   With all my heart.

Exeunt.

*

---

245 *sooth* truth 246 *Heart* by Christ's heart 247 *comfit-maker's* candy-
maker's 250 *sarcenet* flimsy (like the cloth); *surety* warrant, guarantee 251
Finsbury field on the outskirts of London visited by London citizenry (Hotspur accuses Kate of swearing genteel and pious oaths such as sworn by pious
citizens, instead of aristocratic and soldierly oaths) 252 *lady* i.e., noble
254 *protest . . . gingerbread* mealymouthed oaths 255 *velvet . . . citizens*
velvet-trimmed housewives and citizens in Sunday finery 258 *next* easiest;
turn tailor tailors were noted for musical ability, which Hotspur considers effeminate 263 *seal* i.e., with wax seals denoting signatures

∾ **III.2** *Enter the King, Prince of Wales, and others.*

KING

    Lords, give us leave: the Prince of Wales and I

    Must have some private conference; but be near at
      hand,

    For we shall presently have need of you.   *Exeunt Lords.*

    I know not whether God will have it so

    For some displeasing service I have done,

6   That, in his secret doom, out of my blood

7   He'll breed revengement and a scourge for me;

8   But thou dost in thy passages of life

9   Make me believe that thou art only marked

10   For the hot vengeance and the rod of heaven

11   To punish my mistreadings. Tell me else,

12   Could such inordinate and low desires,

13   Such poor, such bare, such lewd, such mean attempts,

    Such barren pleasures, rude society,

15   As thou art matched withal and grafted to,

    Accompany the greatness of thy blood

17   And hold their level with thy princely heart?

PRINCE

    So please your majesty, I would I could

19   Quit all offenses with as clear excuse

20   As well as I am doubtless I can purge

    Myself of many I am charged withal.

22   Yet such extenuation let me beg

23   As, in reproof of many tales devised,

    Which oft the ear of greatness needs must hear

25   By smiling pickthanks and base newsmongers,

III.2 The palace of Henry IV   **6** *doom* judgment   **7** *scourge* punishment   **8** *passages* conduct, actions   **9** *marked* destined   **10** *For* by, in order for   **11** *mistreadings* missteps, mistakes; *else* how else   **12** *inordinate* immoderate, unworthy   **13** *mean attempts* base exploits, undertakings   **15** *grafted* joined   **17** *hold . . . with* be on equal terms with   **19** *Quit* acquit myself of   **20** *doubtless* certain; *purge* cleanse   **22** *extenuation* mitigation, justification   **23** *in reproof* upon disproof   **25** *pickthanks* flatterers; *newsmongers* rumor spreaders, talebearers

I may, for some things true wherein my youth   26
Hath faulty wandered and irregular,
Find pardon on my true submission.   28

KING
God pardon thee! Yet let me wonder, Harry,
At thy affections, which do hold a wing   30
Quite from the flight of all thy ancestors.   31
Thy place in council thou hast rudely lost,   32
Which by thy younger brother is supplied,   33
And art almost an alien to the hearts
Of all the court and princes of my blood.
The hope and expectation of thy time   36
Is ruined, and the soul of every man
Prophetically do forethink thy fall.
Had I so lavish of my presence been,   39
So common-hackneyed in the eyes of men,   40
So stale and cheap to vulgar company,
Opinion, that did help me to the crown,   42
Had still kept loyal to possession   43
And left me in reputeless banishment,   44
A fellow of no mark nor likelihood.   45
By being seldom seen, I could not stir
But, like a comet, I was wondered at;
That men would tell their children, "This is he!"
Others would say, "Where? Which is Bolingbroke?"
And then I stole all courtesy from heaven,   50
And dressed myself in such humility
That I did pluck allegiance from men's hearts,
Loud shouts and salutations from their mouths   53
Even in the presence of the crownèd king.

---

26 *youth* youthfulness   28 *submission* admittance of fault, repentance   30
hold a wing keep (fly a course)   31 *from* away from   32 *council* royal council; *rudely* by violence (Hal was reputed to have punched the Lord Chief Justice, who imprisoned him for it)   33 *supplied* replaced   36 *time* youth   39
lavish free   40 *common-hackneyed* ordinary   42 *Opinion* public opinion
43 *to possession* i.e., that of Richard II, of the throne   44 *reputeless banishment* abandoned exile   45 *mark nor likelihood* name or prospects   50 *stole
all courtesy* appropriated all graciousness   53 *salutations* greetings

Thus did I keep my person fresh and new,
56 My presence, like a robe pontifical,
57 Ne'er seen but wondered at; and so my state,
58 Seldom but sumptuous, showed like a feast
59 And won by rareness such solemnity.
60 The skipping king, he ambled up and down
61 With shallow jesters and rash bavin wits,
62 Soon kindled and soon burnt; carded his state;
Mingled his royalty with cap'ring fools;
64 Had his great name profanèd with their scorns
65 And gave his countenance, against his name,
66 To laugh at gibing boys and stand the push
67 Of every beardless vain comparative;
Grew a companion to the common streets,
69 Enfeoffed himself to popularity;
70 That, being daily swallowed by men's eyes,
71 They surfeited with honey and began
To loathe the taste of sweetness, whereof a little
More than a little is by much too much.
So, when he had occasion to be seen,
75 He was but as the cuckoo is in June,
Heard, not regarded – seen, but with such eyes
77 As, sick and blunted with community,
78 Afford no extraordinary gaze,
79 Such as is bent on sunlike majesty
80 When it shines seldom in admiring eyes;
But rather drowsed and hung their eyelids down,
82 Slept in his face, and rendered such aspect

---

56 *pontifical* i.e., of the pope   57 *state* pomp, presence   58 *Seldom but sumptuous* rare but rich   59 *rareness* infrequency; *solemnity* i.e., of a feast or holiday   60 *skipping king* i.e., Richard II   61 *rash bavin* highly flammable brushwood   62 *carded* mixed (with the lower orders)   64 *profanèd* debased; *their scorns* (the scorns felt for the fools by the populace)   65 *countenance* authority; *against his name* contrary to his lineage and reputation   66 *gibing* taunting; *stand the push* tolerate the impudence   67 *comparative* maker of comparisons   69 *Enfeoffed himself* gave himself up to   71 *surfeited* filled, sated   75 *cuckoo is in June* i.e., nothing unusual   77 *community* commonness, familiarity   78 *extraordinary* wondering   79 *bent* turned   82 *rendered such aspect* showed a face

As cloudy men use to their adversaries,   83
Being with his presence glutted, gorged, and full.
And in that very line, Harry, standest thou;   85
For thou hast lost thy princely privilege
With vile participation. Not an eye   87
But is aweary of thy common sight,
Save mine, which hath desired to see thee more;
Which now doth that I would not have it do –   90
Make blind itself with foolish tenderness.   91

PRINCE
I shall hereafter, my thrice-gracious lord,
Be more myself.

KING   For all the world,
As thou art to this hour was Richard then
When I from France set foot at Ravenspurgh;
And even as I was then is Percy now.
Now, by my scepter, and my soul to boot,   97
He hath more worthy interest to the state   98
Than thou, the shadow of succession;
For of no right, nor color like to right,   100
He doth fill fields with harness in the realm,   101
Turns head against the lion's armèd jaws,   102
And, being no more in debt to years than thou,   103
Leads ancient lords and reverend bishops on   104
To bloody battles and to bruising arms.
What never-dying honor hath he got
Against renownèd Douglas! whose high deeds,   107
Whose hot incursions and great name in arms   108
Holds from all soldiers chief majority   109
And military title capital   110

---

83 *cloudy* sullen (the metaphor draws on that of the king as the sun) 85
very line pattern, tradition   87 *vile participation* consorting with low persons
90 *that* that which   91 *tenderness* tears   97 *to boot* as well   98 *worthy interest to the state* legitimate grounds to rule   100 *color like to* anything resem-
bling   101 *harness* armored men   102 *Turns head* leads an army; *lion's* king's
103 *in debt to years* older   104 *ancient* time-honored   107 *Against* from
fighting   108 *incursions* invasions   109 *from* among; *majority* preeminence
110 *capital* supreme

Through all the kingdoms that acknowledge Christ.
Thrice hath this Hotspur, Mars in swaddling clothes,
This infant warrior, in his enterprises
114   Discomfited great Douglas; ta'en him once,
115   Enlargèd him, and made a friend of him,
116   To fill the mouth of deep defiance up
And shake the peace and safety of our throne.
And what say you to this? Percy, Northumberland,
The Archbishop's grace of York, Douglas, Mortimer
120   Capitulate against us and are up.
But wherefore do I tell these news to thee?
Why, Harry, do I tell thee of my foes,
Which art my nearest and dearest enemy?
124   Thou that art like enough, through vassal fear,
125   Base inclination, and the start of spleen,
To fight against me under Percy's pay,
To dog his heels and curtsy at his frowns,
To show how much thou art degenerate.

PRINCE
Do not think so. You shall not find it so.
130   And God forgive them that so much have swayed
Your majesty's good thoughts away from me.
132   I will redeem all this on Percy's head
133   And, in the closing of some glorious day,
Be bold to tell you that I am your son,
When I will wear a garment all of blood,
136   And stain my favors in a bloody mask,
Which, washed away, shall scour my shame with it.
138   And that shall be the day, whene'er it lights,
That this same child of honor and renown,
140   This gallant Hotspur, this all-praisèd knight,
141   And your unthought-of Harry chance to meet.

---

114 *Discomfited* defeated   115 *Enlargèd* set free   116 *To . . . up* to increase
the sound of defiance   120 *Capitulate* draw up articles; *up* in arms   124 *like*
likely; *vassal* slavish, senile   125 *Base inclination* low tendencies; *spleen* ill
temper   132 *redeem* make up for   133 *closing* end   136 *favors* features
138 *lights* dawns   141 *unthought-of* ill-regarded, ignored

For every honor sitting on his helm,   142
Would they were multitudes, and on my head
My shames redoubled! For the time will come
That I shall make this northern youth exchange
His glorious deeds for my indignities.
Percy is but my factor, good my lord,   147
To engross up glorious deeds on my behalf;   148
And I will call him to so strict account
That he shall render every glory up,   150
Yea, even the slightest worship of his time,   151
Or I will tear the reckoning from his heart.   152
This in the name of God I promise here;
The which if he be pleased I shall perform,   154
I do beseech your majesty may salve   155
The long-grown wounds of my intemperance.   156
If not, the end of life cancels all bands,   157
And I will die a hundred thousand deaths
Ere break the smallest parcel of this vow.

KING
A hundred thousand rebels die in this!   160
Thou shalt have charge and sovereign trust herein.   161
    Enter Blunt.
How now, good Blunt? Thy looks are full of speed.

BLUNT
So hath the business that I come to speak of.
Lord Mortimer of Scotland hath sent word   164
That Douglas and the English rebels met
The eleventh of this month at Shrewsbury.
A mighty and a fearful head they are,   167
If promises be kept on every hand,
As ever offered foul play in a state.

---

142 *helm* helmet, head   147 *factor* agent, instrument   148 *engross* buy
150 *render* give   151 *worship* honor; *time* lifetime   152 *reckoning* amount
owed   154 *he* i.e., God   155 *salve* heal   156 *intemperance* wasteful behavior   157 *bands* bonds, promises   160 *this* this vow   161 *charge* command
164 *Lord Mortimer* a Scottish nobleman unrelated to Edmund Mortimer,
Glendower's son-in-law   167 *head* force

KING

170 The Earl of Westmoreland set forth today;
With him my son, Lord John of Lancaster;
172 For this advertisement is five days old.
On Wednesday next, Harry, you shall set forward;
174 On Thursday we ourselves will march. Our meeting
Is Bridgenorth; and, Harry, you shall march
Through Gloucestershire; by which account,
177 Our business valuèd, some twelve days hence
Our general forces at Bridgenorth shall meet.
Our hands are full of business. Let's away:
180 Advantage feeds him fat while men delay.   *Exeunt.*

*

⁓ **III.3** *Enter Falstaff and Bardolph.*

1 FALSTAFF Bardolph, am I not fallen away vilely since this
2 last action? Do I not bate? Do I not dwindle? Why, my
skin hangs about me like an old lady's loose gown! I am
4 withered like an old applejohn. Well, I'll repent, and that
5 suddenly, while I am in some liking. I shall be out of heart
shortly, and then I shall have no strength to repent. An I
have not forgotten what the inside of a church is made of,
8 I am a peppercorn, a brewer's horse. The inside of a
church! Company, villainous company, hath been the
10 spoil of me.

BARDOLPH Sir John, you are so fretful you cannot live
long.

13 FALSTAFF Why, there is it! Come, sing me a bawdy song;
14 make me merry. I was as virtuously given as a gentle-

---

172 *advertisement* news   174 *meeting* rendezvous   177 *our business valuèd*
depending upon how long our business will take   180 *Advantage* opportunity; *him* himself
III.3 An Eastcheap tavern   1 *fallen* wasted   2 *action* (the robbery); *bate*
shrink   4 *applejohn* shriveled eating apple   5 *suddenly* immediately; *liking* (1)
inclination, (2) good shape   5 *out of heart* (1) disheartened, (2) out of shape
8 *peppercorn* i.e., very small; *brewer's horse* i.e., worn out   13 *there is it* that's
it; *bawdy* lewd   14 *virtuously given* given to good behavior

man need to be, virtuous enough: swore little, diced
not above seven times a week, went to a bawdy house   16
not above once in a quarter of an hour, paid money
that I borrowed three or four times, lived well, and in
good compass; and now I live out of all order, out of all   19
compass.   20

BARDOLPH   Why, you are so fat, Sir John, that you must
needs be out of all compass – out of all reasonable compass, Sir John.

FALSTAFF   Do thou amend thy face, and I'll amend my   24
life. Thou art our admiral, thou bearest the lantern in   25
the poop – but 'tis in the nose of thee. Thou art the   26
Knight of the Burning Lamp.   27

BARDOLPH   Why, Sir John, my face does you no harm.

FALSTAFF   No, I'll be sworn. I make as good use of it as
many a man doth of a death's-head or a memento mori.   30
I never see thy face but I think upon hellfire and Dives   31
that lived in purple; for there he is in his robes, burning, burning. If thou wert any way given to virtue, I
would swear by thy face; my oath should be "By this   34
fire, that's God's angel." But thou art altogether given   35
over, and wert indeed, but for the light in thy face,
the son of utter darkness. When thou ran'st up Gad's
Hill in the night to catch my horse, if I did not think
thou hadst been an ignis fatuus or a ball of wildfire,   39
there's no purchase in money. O, thou art a perpetual   40
triumph, an everlasting bonfire-light! Thou hast saved   41
me a thousand marks in links and torches, walking   42
with thee in the night betwixt tavern and tavern; but

---

16 *bawdy house* house of prostitution   19 *compass* limit, girth   24 *face*
(which is bright red from drinking)   25 *admiral* flagship; *lantern* i.e., for the
fleet to follow   26 *poop* rear deck   27 (Falstaff mockingly compares him to
Amadis, knight of the Burning Sword)   30 *death's-head or a memento mori* a
skull and crossbones, or reminder of death   31 *Dives* the rich man who went
to hell, of Luke 16:19–31   34–35 *By . . . angel* an echo of Exodus 3:2,
Psalms 104:4, or Hebrews 1:7   35–36 *given over* a lost cause   39 *ignis
fatuus* will-o'-the-wisp; *wildfire* fireworks   41 *triumph* torchlight procession
42 *marks* silver coins; *links* flares

44   the sack that thou hast drunk me would have bought
45   me lights as good cheap at the dearest chandler's in Eu-
46   rope. I have maintained that salamander of yours with
      fire any time this two-and-thirty years. God reward me
      for it!

49 BARDOLPH 'Sblood, I would my face were in your belly!

50 FALSTAFF God-a-mercy! so should I be sure to be heart-
      burnt.

      Enter Hostess.

52   How now, Dame Partlet the hen? Have you inquired
      yet who picked my pocket?

    HOSTESS Why, Sir John, what do you think, Sir John?
      Do you think I keep thieves in my house? I have
      searched, I have inquired, so has my husband, man by
57   man, boy by boy, servant by servant. The tithe of a hair
      was never lost in my house before.

59 FALSTAFF Ye lie, hostess. Bardolph was shaved and lost
60   many a hair, and I'll be sworn my pocket was picked.
61   Go to, you are a woman, go!

    HOSTESS Who, I? No; I defy thee! God's light, I was
      never called so in mine own house before!

    FALSTAFF Go to, I know you well enough.

    HOSTESS No, Sir John; you do not know me, Sir John. I
      know you, Sir John. You owe me money, Sir John, and
67   now you pick a quarrel to beguile me of it. I bought
      you a dozen of shirts to your back.

69 FALSTAFF Dowlas, filthy dowlas! I have given them away
70   to bakers' wives; they have made bolters of them.

71 HOSTESS Now, as I am a true woman, holland of eight
72   shillings an ell. You owe money here besides, Sir John,

---

44 *drunk me* drunk off me 45 *as good cheap* as cheap 45 *dearest* most expensive; *chandler's* candlemaker's 46 *salamander* lizard reputed to live in fire
(because so cold-blooded) 49 *I . . . belly* (a proverbial way of retorting to irritating remarks) 52 *Partlet* hen in animal stories 57 *tithe* tenth part
59–60 *lost . . . hair* (1) from shaving, (2) from balding due to syphilis 61
Go to go on, get out of here 67 *beguile* hoodwink 69 *Dowlas* coarse cheap
linen 70 *bolters* flour-sifting cloths 71 *holland* fine lawn linen 72 *ell*
forty-five inches

for your diet and by-drinkings, and money lent you, 73
four-and-twenty pound.

FALSTAFF   He had his part of it; let him pay. 75

HOSTESS   He? Alas, he is poor; he hath nothing.

FALSTAFF   How? Poor? Look upon his face. What call
you rich? Let them coin his nose, let them coin his
cheeks. I'll not pay a denier. What, will you make a 79
younker of me? Shall I not take mine ease in mine inn 80
but I shall have my pocket picked? I have lost a seal ring
of my grandfather's worth forty mark.

HOSTESS   O Jesu, I have heard the prince tell him, I
know not how oft, that that ring was copper!

FALSTAFF   How? the prince is a jack, a sneak-up. 'Sblood, 85
an he were here, I would cudgel him like a dog if he 86
would say so. 87

*Enter the Prince [and Peto], marching, and Falstaff
meets them, playing upon his truncheon like a fife.*

How now, lad? Is the wind in that door, i' faith? Must 88
we all march?

BARDOLPH   Yea, two and two, Newgate fashion. 90

HOSTESS   My lord, I pray you hear me.

PRINCE   What say'st thou, Mistress Quickly? How doth
thy husband? I love him well; he is an honest man.

HOSTESS   Good my lord, hear me.

FALSTAFF   Prithee let her alone and list to me.

PRINCE   What say'st thou, Jack?

FALSTAFF   The other night I fell asleep here behind the
arras and had my pocket picked. This house is turned
bawdy house; they pick pockets.

PRINCE   What didst thou lose, Jack? *100*

---

73 *by-drinkings* i.e., between meals   75 *He* i.e., Bardolph   79 *denier* one
twelfth of a French sou, a very small coin   80 *younker* fool, gull, greenhorn;
ease relaxation   85 *jack* knave, rascal; *sneak-up* sneak   86 *cudgel him* beat
him with a stick   87 **s.d.** *truncheon* club, stick   88 *Is . . . door* is that the way
the wind blows   90 *Newgate fashion* chained together like inmates of the London prison

FALSTAFF Wilt thou believe me, Hal, three or four bonds
of forty pound apiece and a seal ring of my grandfather's.

104 PRINCE A trifle, some eightpenny matter.

HOSTESS So I told him, my lord, and I said I heard your
grace say so; and, my lord, he speaks most vilely of you,
like a foulmouthed man as he is, and said he would
cudgel you.

PRINCE What! he did not?

110 HOSTESS There's neither faith, truth, nor womanhood
in me else.

112 FALSTAFF There's no more faith in thee than in a stewed
113 prune, nor no more truth in thee than in a drawn fox;
114 and for womanhood, Maid Marian may be the deputy's
wife of the ward to thee. Go, you thing, go!

HOSTESS Say, what thing? what thing?

FALSTAFF What thing? Why, a thing to thank God on.

HOSTESS I am no thing to thank God on, I would thou
119 shouldst know it! I am an honest man's wife, and, set-
120 ting thy knighthood aside, thou art a knave to call
me so.

FALSTAFF Setting thy womanhood aside, thou art a beast
to say otherwise.

HOSTESS Say, what beast, thou knave, thou?

FALSTAFF What beast? Why, an otter.

PRINCE An otter, Sir John? Why an otter?

FALSTAFF Why? She's neither fish nor flesh; a man knows
128 not where to have her.

HOSTESS Thou art an unjust man in saying so. Thou or
130 any man knows where to have me, thou knave, thou!

PRINCE Thou say'st true, hostess, and he slanders thee
most grossly.

---

104 *trifle* cheap thing   112–13 *stewed prune* associated with brothels   113
a drawn fox hunted and drawn from cover   114–15 *Maid Marian . . . thee*
compared to you, Maid Marian (a disreputable woman of folklore) would be
respectable   119–20 *setting . . . aside* the fact that you are a knight notwith-
standing, not wishing to offend your knighthood   128 *have* take sexual possession of

HOSTESS   So he doth you, my lord, and said this other
day you ought him a thousand pound.   134

PRINCE   Sirrah, do I owe you a thousand pound?

FALSTAFF   A thousand pound, Hal? A million! Thy love is
worth a million; thou owest me thy love.

HOSTESS   Nay, my lord, he called you Jack and said he
would cudgel you.

FALSTAFF   Did I, Bardolph?   140

BARDOLPH   Indeed, Sir John, you said so.

FALSTAFF   Yea, if he said my ring was copper.

PRINCE   I say 'tis copper. Darest thou be as good as thy
word now?

FALSTAFF   Why, Hal, thou knowest, as thou art but man,
I dare; but as thou art prince, I fear thee as I fear the
roaring of the lion's whelp.   147

PRINCE   And why not as the lion?

FALSTAFF   The king himself is to be feared as the lion.
Dost thou think I'll fear thee as I fear thy father? Nay,   150
an I do, I pray God my girdle break.   151

PRINCE   O, if it should, how would thy guts fall about
thy knees! But, sirrah, there's no room for faith, truth,
nor honesty in this bosom of thine. It is all filled up
with guts and midriff. Charge an honest woman with
picking thy pocket? Why, thou whoreson, impudent,
embossed rascal, if there were anything in thy pocket   157
but tavern reckonings, memorandums of bawdy   158
houses, and one poor pennyworth of sugar candy to
make thee long-winded – if thy pocket were enriched   160
with any other injuries but these, I am a villain. And   161
yet you will stand to it; you will not pocket up wrong.   162
Art thou not ashamed?

FALSTAFF   Dost thou hear, Hal? Thou knowest in the
state of innocency Adam fell, and what should poor

---

134 *ought* owed; *pound* currency   147 *whelp* offspring, cub   151 *girdle* belt-
like article of dress   157 *embossed* swollen; *rascal* lean deer   158 *reckonings*
bills; *memorandums* mementos   161 *injuries* things you claim to have lost
162 *stand to it* insist; *pocket up* endure silently

Jack Falstaff do in the days of villainy? Thou seest I have
more flesh than another man, and therefore more
frailty. You confess then, you picked my pocket?

PRINCE   It appears so by the story.

170 FALSTAFF   Hostess, I forgive thee. Go make ready breakfast. Love thy husband, look to thy servants, cherish
172 thy guests. Thou shalt find me tractable to any honest
173 reason. Thou seest I am pacified still. Nay, prithee be
gone.   *Exit Hostess.*
Now, Hal, to the news at court. For the robbery, lad –
how is that answered?

PRINCE   O my sweet beef, I must still be good angel to
thee. The money is paid back again.

FALSTAFF   O, I do not like that paying back! 'Tis a double
180 labor.

PRINCE   I am good friends with my father, and may do
anything.

183 FALSTAFF   Rob me the exchequer the first thing thou
184 doest, and do it with unwashed hands too.

BARDOLPH   Do, my lord.

186 PRINCE   I have procured thee, Jack, a charge of foot.

187 FALSTAFF   I would it had been of horse. Where shall I
188 find one that can steal well? O for a fine thief of the age
189 of two-and-twenty or thereabouts! I am heinously un-
190 provided. Well, God be thanked for these rebels. They
offend none but the virtuous. I laud them, I praise
them.

PRINCE   Bardolph!

BARDOLPH   My lord?

PRINCE
Go bear this letter to Lord John of Lancaster,
To my brother John; this to my Lord of Westmoreland.
                                         [Exit Bardolph.]

---

172 *tractable* agreeable to, appeased by   173 *still* always   183 *exchequer*
treasury   184 *unwashed hands* without delay   186 *charge of foot* command
of a troop of infantry   187 *horse* cavalry   188 *one* a partner in crime   189
two-and-twenty i.e., Hal's age   189–90 *heinously unprovided* grievously un-
prepared   190 *God be thanked* (Falstaff views the war as an opportunity)

Go, Peto, to horse, to horse; for thou and I
Have thirty miles to ride yet ere dinnertime.

          [Exit Peto.]

Jack, meet me tomorrow in the Temple Hall   199
At two o'clock in the afternoon.   *200*
There shalt thou know thy charge, and there receive
Money and order for their furniture.   202
The land is burning; Percy stands on high;
And either we or they must lower lie.   *[Exit.]*

FALSTAFF
Rare words! brave world! Hostess, my breakfast, come.   205
O, I could wish this tavern were my drum!   *Exit.*

        *

∾ **IV.1** *[Enter Hotspur, Worcester, and Douglas.]*

HOTSPUR
Well said, my noble Scot. If speaking truth
In this fine age were not thought flattery,
Such attribution should the Douglas have   3
As not a soldier of this season's stamp   4
Should go so general current through the world.   5
By God, I cannot flatter, I do defy   6
The tongues of soothers! but a braver place   7
In my heart's love hath no man than yourself.
Nay, task me to my word; approve me, lord.   9

DOUGLAS
Thou art the king of honor.   *10*
No man so potent breathes upon the ground   11
But I will beard him.   12

  Enter one with letters.

---

199 *Temple Hall* one of the Inns of Court (the law courts and schools)   **202**
furniture equipment   **205** *Rare* brave, splendid

 IV.1 The rebel camp at Shrewsbury   **3** *attribution* tribute   **4** *stamp*
coinage, pattern   **5** *go . . . current* be so universally esteemed and accepted
6 *defy* despise   **7** *soothers* flatterers; *braver* better   **9** *task* test, keep; *approve*
put to the test   **11** *potent* powerful   **12** *But* but that; *beard* defy, best

HOTSPUR   Do so, and 'tis well. –
  What letters hast thou there? – I can but thank you.
MESSENGER
  These letters come from your father.
HOTSPUR
  Letters from him? Why comes he not himself?
MESSENGER
16 He cannot come, my lord; he is grievous sick.
HOTSPUR
17 Zounds! how has he the leisure to be sick
  In such a jostling time? Who leads his power?
19 Under whose government come they along?
MESSENGER
20 His letters bears his mind, not I, my lord.
WORCESTER
21 I prithee tell me, doth he keep his bed?
MESSENGER
  He did, my lord, four days ere I set forth,
  And at the time of my departure thence
24 He was much feared by his physicians.
WORCESTER
25 I would the state of time had first been whole
  Ere he by sickness had been visited.
27 His health was never better worth than now.
HOTSPUR
  Sick now? droop now? This sickness doth infect
  The very lifeblood of our enterprise.
30 'Tis catching hither, even to our camp.
  He writes me here that inward sickness –
32 And that his friends by deputation could not
33 So soon be drawn; nor did he think it meet
  To lay so dangerous and dear a trust
35 On any soul removed but on his own.

---

16 *grievous* grievously, terribly   17 *Zounds* God's wounds   19 *government* command   21 *keep* keep to   24 *feared* feared for   25 *time* the times; *whole* peaceful, ordered   27 *better worth* worth more   32 *deputation* deputies   33 *drawn* assembled; *meet* suitable   35 *removed . . . own* other than himself

Yet doth he give us bold advertisement,   36
That with our small conjunction we should on,   37
To see how fortune is disposed to us;   38
For, as he writes, there is no quailing now,   39
Because the king is certainly possessed   40
Of all our purposes. What say you to it?

WORCESTER
Your father's sickness is a maim to us.   42

HOTSPUR
A perilous gash, a very limb lopped off.
And yet, in faith, it is not! His present want   44
Seems more than we shall find it. Were it good
To set the exact wealth of all our states   46
All at one cast? to set so rich a main   47
On the nice hazard of one doubtful hour?   48
It were not good; for therein should we read   49
The very bottom and the soul of hope,   50
The very list, the very utmost bound   51
Of all our fortunes.

DOUGLAS   Faith, and so we should.
Where now remains a sweet reversion,   53
We may boldly spend upon the hope of what
Is to come in.
A comfort of retirement lives in this.   56

HOTSPUR
A rendezvous, a home to fly unto,
If that the devil and mischance look big   58
Upon the maidenhead of our affairs.   59

---

36 *advertisement* advice   37 *conjunction* conjoined forces; *on* go on (to fight)
38 *fortune* fate, divine will   39 *quailing* backing down   40 *possessed* in-
formed   42 *maim* injury   44 *want* absence   46 *states* (1) fortunes, (2)
estates   47 *cast* throw of the dice; *main* stake, army   48 *nice* delicate,
chancy; *hazard* (1) chance, peril, (2) dice game   49 *read* learn   50 *bottom*
basis   51 *list* limit; *bound* boundary   53 *reversion* future prospects, inheritance   56 *retirement* something to fall back upon   58 *big* threateningly   59
maidenhead i.e., beginning (literally hymen, the physical marker of female
virginity)

WORCESTER

60   But yet I would your father had been here.

61   The quality and hair of our attempt

62   Brooks no division. It will be thought

    By some that know not why he is away,

64   That wisdom, loyalty, and mere dislike

    Of our proceedings kept the earl from hence.

    And think how such an apprehension

67   May turn the tide of fearful faction

68   And breed a kind of question in our cause.

69   For well you know we of the off'ring side

70   Must keep aloof from strict arbitrament,

71   And stop all sightholes, every loop from whence

    The eye of reason may pry in upon us.

73   This absence of your father's draws a curtain

    That shows the ignorant a kind of fear

75   Before not dreamt of.

HOTSPUR   You strain too far.

    I rather of his absence make this use:

77   It lends a luster and more great opinion,

78   A larger dare to our great enterprise,

    Than if the earl were here; for men must think,

80   If we, without his help, can make a head

    To push against a kingdom, with his help

    We shall o'erturn it topsy-turvy down.

83   Yet all goes well; yet all our joints are whole.

DOUGLAS

    As heart can think. There is not such a word

    Spoke of in Scotland as this term of fear.

      Enter Sir Richard Vernon.

HOTSPUR

    My cousin Vernon! welcome, by my soul.

---

61 *hair* nature   **62** *Brooks* tolerates   **64** *loyalty* i.e., to the king; *mere* utter **67** *fearful* timid; *faction* support   **68** *question* doubt   **69** *off'ring* challenging **70** *arbitrament* investigation, scrutiny   **71** *sightholes* loopholes   **73** *draws* opens   **75** *strain* reach, exaggerate   **77** *luster* shine; *opinion* prestige   **78** *dare* daring   **80** *head* force, army   **83** *joints* limbs

VERNON
   Pray God my news be worth a welcome, lord.
   The Earl of Westmoreland, seven thousand strong,
   Is marching hitherwards; with him Prince John.

HOTSPUR
   No harm. What more?   *90*

VERNON   And further, I have learned
   The king himself in person is set forth,
   Or hitherwards intended speedily,   *92*
   With strong and mighty preparation.

HOTSPUR
   He shall be welcome too. Where is his son,
   The nimble-footed madcap Prince of Wales,
   And his comrades, that daffed the world aside   *96*
   And bid it pass?   *97*

VERNON   All furnished, all in arms;
   All plumed like estridges that with the wind   *98*
   Bated like eagles having lately bathed;   *99*
   Glittering in golden coats like images;   *100*
   As full of spirit as the month of May
   And gorgeous as the sun at midsummer;
   Wanton as youthful goats, wild as young bulls.   *103*
   I saw young Harry with his beaver on,   *104*
   His cuisses on his thighs, gallantly armed,   *105*
   Risc from the ground like feathered Mercury,   *106*
   And vaulted with such ease into his seat   *107*
   As if an angel dropped down from the clouds
   To turn and wind a fiery Pegasus   *109*
   And witch the world with noble horsemanship.   *110*

---

92 *intended* i.e., to come **96** *daffed* (1) put aside, (2) tipped his hat at **97** *furnished* armed, equipped **98** *estridges* ostriches **99** *Bated* flapped wings **100** *coats* (of armor); *images* gilded statues **103** *Wanton* frisky, sportive **104** *beaver* armor **105** *cuisses* thigh armor **106** *Mercury* messenger of the gods (with winged feet) **107** *vaulted* jumped **109** *Pegasus* winged horse of Greek mythology **110** *witch* bewitch, charm

HOTSPUR

No more, no more! Worse than the sun in March,
112   This praise doth nourish agues. Let them come.
113   They come like sacrifices in their trim,
114   And to the fire-eyed maid of smoky war
     All hot and bleeding will we offer them.
116   The mailèd Mars shall on his altar sit
     Up to the ears in blood. I am on fire
118   To hear this rich reprisal is so nigh,
119   And yet not ours. Come, let me taste my horse,
120   Who is to bear me like a thunderbolt
     Against the bosom of the Prince of Wales.
     Harry to Harry shall, hot horse to horse,
     Meet, and ne'er part till one drop down a corpse.
     O that Glendower were come!

VERNON   There is more news.

     I learned in Worcester, as I rode along,
126   He cannot draw his power this fourteen days.

DOUGLAS

     That's the worst tidings that I hear of yet.

WORCESTER

     Ay, by my faith, that bears a frosty sound.

HOTSPUR

129   What may the king's whole battle reach unto?

VERNON

130   To thirty thousand.

HOTSPUR   Forty let it be.

     My father and Glendower being both away,
132   The powers of us may serve so great a day.
     Come, let us take a muster speedily.
     Doomsday is near. Die all, die merrily.

---

112 *agues* shivery fear (believed to be caused by the vapors drawn by the spring sun) 113 *trim* decoration, finery 114 *maid* the goddess of war, Bellona 116 *mailèd* i.e., chain-mail-wearing; *Mars* god of war 118 *reprisal* prize, booty 119 *taste* feel 126 *draw* muster, gather; *this* for 129 *battle* army 132 *may serve* must be adequate to serve

DOUGLAS
Talk not of dying. I am out of fear   135
Of death or death's hand for this one half-year. *Exeunt.*

*

∾ **IV.2** *Enter Falstaff and Bardolph.*

FALSTAFF   Bardolph, get thee before to Coventry; fill me   1
a bottle of sack. Our soldiers shall march through.
We'll to Sutton Co'fil' tonight.   3
BARDOLPH   Will you give me money, captain?
FALSTAFF   Lay out, lay out.   5
BARDOLPH   This bottle makes an angel.   6
FALSTAFF   An if it do, take it for thy labor; an if it make   7
twenty, take them all; I'll answer the coinage. Bid my   8
lieutenant Peto meet me at town's end.
BARDOLPH   I will, captain. Farewell.   *Exit.*   10
FALSTAFF   If I be not ashamed of my soldiers, I am a
soused gurnet. I have misused the king's press   12
damnably. I have got, in exchange of a hundred and   13
fifty soldiers, three hundred and odd pounds. I press
me none but good householders, yeomen's sons; in-   15
quire me out contracted bachelors, such as had been   16
asked twice on the banns – such a commodity of warm   17
slaves as had as lieve hear the devil as a drum, such as   18

---

135 *out of* free from
   IV.2 The road to Coventry   **1** *get thee before* go ahead   **3** *Sutton Co'fil'*
(Sutton Coldfield is twenty miles beyond Coventry)   **5** *Lay out* pay for it
yourself   **6** *an angel* ten shillings (that you owe me, that I've spent for you)
7 *An . . . do* (Falstaff pretends that "makes" means "creates"); *labor* effort   **8**
answer answer for, be responsible for (as if coinage were privately, illegally
minted)   **12** *soused gurnet* pickled fish (with a large head and a slender
body – i.e., the contrary of Falstaff); *press* the right of conscription (drafting)
13 *in exchange of* instead of (for allowing men to buy their way out of being
drafted)   **15** *good householders* wealthy homeowners; *yeomen* small freehold-
ers   **16** *contracted* engaged to be married   **17** *banns* public announcements,
made on three Sundays, of an intent to marry   **18** *lieve* rather

19 fear the report of a caliver worse than a struck fowl or a
20 hurt wild duck. I pressed me none but such toasts-and-
butter, with hearts in their bellies no bigger than pins'
heads, and they have bought out their services; and
23 now my whole charge consists of ancients, corporals,
24 lieutenants, gentlemen of companies – slaves as ragged
25 as Lazarus in the painted cloth, where the glutton's
dogs licked his sores; and such as indeed were never sol-
27 diers, but discarded unjust servingmen, younger sons
28 to younger brothers, revolted tapsters, and ostlers
29 trade-fallen; the cankers of a calm world and a long
30 peace; ten times more dishonorable ragged than an old
31 fazed ancient; and such have I to fill up the rooms of
them as have bought out their services that you would
33 think that I had a hundred and fifty tattered prodigals
34 lately come from swine-keeping, from eating draff and
husks. A mad fellow met me on the way, and told me I
36 had unloaded all the gibbets and pressed the dead bodies. No eye hath seen such scarecrows. I'll not march
38 through Coventry with them, that's flat. Nay, and the
39 villains march wide betwixt the legs, as if they had
40 gyves on, for indeed I had the most of them out of
prison. There's not a shirt and a half in all my company,
and the half-shirt is two napkins tacked together and
thrown over the shoulders like a herald's coat without
sleeves; and the shirt, to say the truth, stol'n from my
host at Saint Alban's, or the red-nose innkeeper of Dav-

---

19 *caliver* musket 20–21 *toasts-and-butter* cowards, sissies (too elegant to
fight) 23 *charge* command; *ancients* ensigns, or standard-bearers (Falstaff
has signed on men at more than the usual numbers of officers in order to col-
lect – and pocket – their higher pay) 24 *gentlemen of companies* volunteers
25 *Lazarus* the beggar; *painted cloth* a wall decoration 27 *unjust* dishonest;
younger sons i.e., with no hope of inheritance 28 *revolted* run away from
their apprenticeships 28–29 *ostlers trade-fallen* horse handlers whose business has fallen off 29 *cankers* worms 31 *fazed ancient* frayed flag; *fill up the
rooms* take the place of 33 *prodigals* i.e., prodigal sons; see Luke 15:15–16
34 *draff* pig swill 36 *gibbets* structures for hanging people 38 *flat* for sure
39 *wide . . . legs* with their legs apart 40 *gyves* prisoner's chains

entry. But that's all one; they'll find linen enough on   46
every hedge.

Enter the Prince and the Lord of Westmoreland.

PRINCE   How now, blown Jack? How now, quilt?   48

FALSTAFF   What, Hal? How now, mad wag? What a devil
dost thou in Warwickshire? My good Lord of West-   50
moreland, I cry you mercy. I thought your honor had   51
already been at Shrewsbury.

WESTMORELAND   Faith, Sir John, 'tis more than time
that I were there, and you too, but my powers are there   54
already. The king, I can tell you, looks for us all. We
must away all night.   56

FALSTAFF   Tut, never fear me: I am as vigilant as a cat to   57
steal cream.

PRINCE   I think, to steal cream indeed, for thy theft hath
already made thee butter. But tell me, Jack, whose fel-   60
lows are these that come after?

FALSTAFF   Mine, Hal, mine.

PRINCE   I did never see such pitiful rascals.

FALSTAFF   Tut, tut! good enough to toss; food for pow-   64
der, food for powder. They'll fill a pit as well as better.   65
Tush, man, mortal men, mortal men.   66

WESTMORELAND   Ay, but, Sir John, methinks they are
exceeding poor and bare – too beggarly.

FALSTAFF   Faith, for their poverty, I know not where they
had that, and for their bareness, I am sure they never   70
learned that of me.

PRINCE   No, I'll be sworn, unless you call three fingers in   72
the ribs bare. But, sirrah, make haste. Percy is already in
the field.   *Exit.*

FALSTAFF   What, is the king encamped?

46–47 *linen . . . hedge* washed clothes were dried on hedges 48 *blown*
swollen (with office); *quilt* a soldier's quilted jacket was called a jack 51 *cry
you mercy* beg your pardon 54 *powers* forces, soldiers 56 *must away* march
57 *fear* worry about 64 *toss* i.e., on a pike (a sharp pole) 64–65 *powder*
gunpowder (i.e., cannon fodder) 65 *better* i.e., their betters 66 *Tush* a
scoffing term 72 *fingers* a finger was three quarters of an inch

WESTMORELAND   He is, Sir John. I fear we shall stay too
    long.   *[Exit.]*
78 FALSTAFF   Well, to the latter end of a fray and the begin-
79   ning of a feast fits a dull fighter and a keen guest.
                                                        Exit.

*

∽ **IV.3** *Enter Hotspur, Worcester, Douglas, Vernon.*

HOTSPUR
    We'll fight with him tonight.
WORCESTER   It may not be.
DOUGLAS
2   You give him then advantage.
VERNON   Not a whit.
HOTSPUR
3   Why say you so? Looks he not for supply?
VERNON
    So do we.
HOTSPUR   His is certain, ours is doubtful.
WORCESTER
    Good cousin, be advised; stir not tonight.
VERNON
    Do not, my lord.
DOUGLAS   You do not counsel well.
    You speak it out of fear and cold heart.
VERNON
    Do me no slander, Douglas. By my life –
    And I dare well maintain it with my life –
10 If well-respected honor bid me on,
11 I hold as little counsel with weak fear
    As you, my lord, or any Scot that this day lives.
    Let it be seen tomorrow in the battle

---

78 *latter end* finish; *fray* fight   79 *keen* eager
    IV.3 The rebel camp   2 *then* i.e., if you wait; *whit* small amount   3 *sup-*
ply reinforcements   10 *well-respected* well-considered; *on* i.e., to fight   11
counsel traffic, company

Which of us fears.

DOUGLAS   Yea, or tonight.

VERNON   Content.

HOTSPUR

Tonight, say I.

VERNON

Come, come, it may not be. I wonder much,

Being men of such great leading as you are,   17

That you foresee not what impediments

Drag back our expedition. Certain horse   19

Of my cousin Vernon's are not yet come up.   20

Your uncle Worcester's horse came but today;

And now their pride and mettle is asleep,   22

Their courage with hard labor tame and dull,

That not a horse is half the half of himself.

HOTSPUR

So are the horses of the enemy

In general journey-bated and brought low.   26

The better part of ours are full of rest.

WORCESTER

The number of the king exceedeth ours.

For God's sake, cousin, stay till all come in.

The trumpet sounds a parley.

Enter Sir Walter Blunt.

BLUNT

I come with gracious offers from the king,   30

If you vouchsafe me hearing and respect.   31

HOTSPUR

Welcome, Sir Walter Blunt, and would to God

You were of our determination.   33

Some of us love you well; and even those some

Envy your great deservings and good name,   35

Because you are not of our quality,   36

---

17 *leading* leadership   19 *horse* i.e., cavalry   22 *pride and mettle* spirit   26 *journey-bated* worn out from traveling   31 *vouchsafe* grant, give; *respect* attention   33 *determination* mind, opinion   35 *deservings* reputation, honors   36 *quality* party, number

But stand against us like an enemy.

BLUNT

38 And God defend but still I should stand so,
39 So long as out of limit and true rule
40 You stand against anointed majesty.
But to my charge. The king hath sent to know
42 The nature of your griefs, and whereupon
You conjure from the breast of civil peace
Such bold hostility, teaching his duteous land
Audacious cruelty. If that the king
46 Have any way your good deserts forgot,
Which he confesseth to be manifold,
He bids you name your griefs, and with all speed
You shall have your desires with interest,
50 And pardon absolute for yourself and these
51 Herein misled by your suggestion.

HOTSPUR

The king is kind, and well we know the king
Knows at what time to promise, when to pay.
My father and my uncle and myself
Did give him that same royalty he wears;
56 And when he was not six-and-twenty strong,
57 Sick in the world's regard, wretched and low,
58 A poor unminded outlaw sneaking home,
My father gave him welcome to the shore;
60 And when he heard him swear and vow to God
He came but to be Duke of Lancaster,
62 To sue his livery and beg his peace,
63 With tears of innocency and terms of zeal,
My father, in kind heart and pity moved,
Swore him assistance, and performed it too.
Now when the lords and barons of the realm

---

38 *defend* forbid   39 *limit* bounds of allegiance and law; *rule* law, rulership
42 *griefs* grievances   46 *deserts* deservings, what is owed to   51 *suggestion* in-
stigation   56 *six-and-twenty* i.e., twenty-six men   57 *Sick* unworthy, ill-es-
teemed   58 *unminded* ignominious, ignored   62 *sue his livery* sue for his
inheritance (confiscated by Richard II)   63 *zeal* sincerity

Perceived Northumberland did lean to him,   67
The more and less came in with cap and knee;   68
Met him in boroughs, cities, villages,
Attended him on bridges, stood in lanes,   70
Laid gifts before him, proffered him their oaths,
Gave him their heirs as pages, followed him   72
Even at the heels in golden multitudes.   73
He presently, as greatness knows itself,   74
Steps me a little higher than his vow   75
Made to my father, while his blood was poor,   76
Upon the naked shore at Ravenspurgh;
And now, forsooth, takes on him to reform   78
Some certain edicts and some strait decrees   79
That lie too heavy on the commonwealth;   80
Cries out upon abuses, seems to weep   81
Over his country's wrongs; and by this face,   82
This seeming brow of justice, did he win   83
The hearts of all that he did angle for;   84
Proceeded further – cut me off the heads   85
Of all the favorites that the absent king   86
In deputation left behind him here   87
When he was personal in the Irish war.   88

BLUNT
Tut! I came not to hear this.

HOTSPUR   Then to the point.
In short time after, he deposed the king;   90
Soon after that deprived him of his life;
And in the neck of that tasked the whole state;   92

------

67 *lean to* favor   68 *more and less* greater and lesser nobles; *cap and knee* i.e.,
with cap off and bended knee   70 *Attended him* waited for   72 *pages* young
servants, attendants   73 *golden* (1) richly dressed, (2) promising   74 *knows
itself* feels its own strength   75 *Steps me* goes beyond; *vow* (promise to seek
no more than his inheritance)   76 *blood* spirit; *poor* unambitious, without
hope   78 *forsooth* indeed; *takes on him* takes it upon himself   79 *strait* strict
81 *Cries out upon* protests   82 *face* (1) appearance, (2) pretext   83 *seeming
brow* pretense, face   84 *angle* fish   85 *cut me off* cut off   86 *favorites* i.e., of
the king   87 *In deputation* as deputies   88 *personal* in person   92 *in the
neck of* immediately after; *tasked* taxed

93   To make that worse, suffered his kinsman March
94   (Who is, if every owner were well placed,
95   Indeed his king) to be engaged in Wales,
96   There without ransom to lie forfeited;
97   Disgraced me in my happy victories,
98   Sought to entrap me by intelligence;
99   Rated mine uncle from the council board;
100   In rage dismissed my father from the court;
     Broke oath on oath, committed wrong on wrong;
     And in conclusion drove us to seek out
103   This head of safety, and withal to pry
     Into his title, the which we find
105   Too indirect for long continuance.

BLUNT
   Shall I return this answer to the king?

HOTSPUR
   Not so, Sir Walter. We'll withdraw awhile.
108   Go to the king; and let there be impawned
109   Some surety for a safe return again,
110   And in the morning early shall mine uncle
111   Bring him our purposes; and so farewell.

BLUNT
112   I would you would accept of grace and love.

HOTSPUR
   And may be so we shall.

BLUNT   Pray God you do.   *Exeunt.*

*

---

93 *suffered* allowed   **94** *if . . . placed* if everyone were in their proper places   **95** *engaged* held as hostage   **96** *forfeited* unreclaimed   **97** *happy* fortunate   **98** *intelligence* spying   **99** *Rated* scolded   **103** *head of safety* army of protection; *withal* at the same time   **105** *indirect* i.e., unlawfully acquired; *continuance* possession, duration   **108** *impawned* pledged   **109** *surety* guarantee   **111** *purposes* intentions, proposals, answer   **112** *accept of* accept (the king's forgiveness)

∾ **IV.4** *Enter the Archbishop of York and Sir Michael.*

ARCHBISHOP

Hie, good Sir Michael; bear this sealèd brief   1
With wingèd haste to the lord marshal;   2
This to my cousin Scroop; and all the rest   3
To whom they are directed. If you knew
How much they do import, you would make haste.

SIR MICHAEL

My good lord,
I guess their tenor.   7

ARCHBISHOP   Like enough you do.
Tomorrow, good Sir Michael, is a day
Wherein the fortune of ten thousand men
Must bide the touch; for, sir, at Shrewsbury,   10
As I am truly given to understand,
The king with mighty and quick-raisèd power
Meets with Lord Harry; and I fear, Sir Michael,
What with the sickness of Northumberland,
Whose power was in the first proportion,   15
And what with Owen Glendower's absence thence,
Who with them was a rated sinew too   17
And comes not in, overruled by prophecies –
I fear the power of Percy is too weak
To wage an instant trial with the king.   20

SIR MICHAEL

Why, my good lord, you need not fear;
There is Douglas and Lord Mortimer.

ARCHBISHOP

No, Mortimer is not there.

IV.4 York, the archbishop's palace   **1** *Hie* go, hurry; *brief* letter   **2** *wingèd*
i.e., like Mercury, messenger of the gods; *lord marshal* i.e., Thomas Mow-
bray, son of the Duke of Norfolk, an enemy of the king   **3** *This* this other
letter; *Scroop* i.e., perhaps Sir Stephen Scroop of *Richard II*, III.2, or Lord
Scroop of *Henry V,* II.2   **7** *tenor* content   **10** *bide the touch* withstand the
test   **15** *first proportion* greater magnitude   **17** *rated sinew* valued source of
strength, support   **20** *wage* risk; *instant* immediate

SIR MICHAEL

But there is Mordake, Vernon, Lord Harry Percy,
25 And there is my Lord of Worcester, and a head
Of gallant warriors, noble gentlemen.

ARCHBISHOP

And so there is; but yet the king hath drawn
The special head of all the land together –
The Prince of Wales, Lord John of Lancaster,
30 The noble Westmoreland and warlike Blunt,
31 And many more corrivals and dear men
Of estimation and command in arms.

SIR MICHAEL

Doubt not, my lord, they shall be well opposed.

ARCHBISHOP

I hope no less, yet needful 'tis to fear;
And, to prevent the worst, Sir Michael, speed.
36 For if Lord Percy thrive not, ere the king
Dismiss his power, he means to visit us,
38 For he hath heard of our confederacy,
39 And 'tis but wisdom to make strong against him.
40 Therefore make haste. I must go write again
To other friends; and so farewell, Sir Michael.   *Exeunt.*

∗

∾ **V.1** *Enter the King, Prince of Wales, Lord John of Lancaster, Sir Walter Blunt, Falstaff.*

KING

How bloodily the sun begins to peer
2 Above yon bulky hill! The day looks pale
3 At his distemp'rature.

PRINCE   The southern wind
4 Doth play the trumpet to his purposes

---

25 *head* force 31 *corrivals* allies; *dear* valued 36 *thrive* succeed 38 *confederacy* alliance 39 *make strong* prepare ourselves

V.1 Shrewsbury, the royal camp 2 *bulky* looming 3 *distemp'prature* unhealthy appearance 4 *trumpet* trumpeter, herald; *his* i.e., the sun's

And by his hollow whistling in the leaves
Foretells a tempest and a blust'ring day.

KING

Then with the losers let it sympathize,
For nothing can seem foul to those that win.

The trumpet sounds. Enter Worcester [and Vernon].

How now, my Lord of Worcester? 'Tis not well
That you and I should meet upon such terms   *10*
As now we meet. You have deceived our trust
And made us doff our easy robes of peace   *12*
To crush our old limbs in ungentle steel.
This is not well, my lord; this is not well.
What say you to it? Will you again unknit
This churlish knot of all-abhorrèd war,
And move in that obedient orb again   *17*
Where you did give a fair and natural light,
And be no more an exhaled meteor,   *19*
A prodigy of fear, and a portent   *20*
Of broachèd mischief to the unborn times?   *21*

WORCESTER

Hear me, my liege.
For mine own part, I could be well content
To entertain the lag-end of my life   *24*
With quiet hours, for I do protest
I have not sought the day of this dislike.   *26*

KING

You have not sought it! How comes it then?

FALSTAFF

Rebellion lay in his way, and he found it.

PRINCE

Peace, chewet, peace!   *29*

WORCESTER

It pleased your majesty to turn your looks   *30*

---

12 *doff* cast off, remove; *easy* comfortable   **17** *orb* orbit (the king's subjects
are compared to revolving planets)   **19** *exhaled meteor* (meteors were
thought to be drawn up by the sun and ill omens)   **20** *prodigy* sign, omen
21 *broachèd* launched, begun   **24** *entertain* occupy; *lag-end* latter finish   **26**
dislike discord, unrest   **29** *chewet* chatterer (jackdaw)

31   Of favor from myself and all our house;
32   And yet I must remember you, my lord,
      We were the first and dearest of your friends.
34   For you my staff of office did I break
35   In Richard's time, and posted day and night
      To meet you on the way and kiss your hand
37   When yet you were in place and in account
      Nothing so strong and fortunate as I.
      It was myself, my brother, and his son
40   That brought you home and boldly did outdare
      The dangers of the time. You swore to us,
      And you did swear that oath at Doncaster,
43   That you did nothing purpose 'gainst the state,
44   Nor claim no further than your new-fallen right,
      The seat of Gaunt, dukedom of Lancaster.
      To this we swore our aid. But in short space
      It rained down fortune show'ring on your head,
      And such a flood of greatness fell on you –
      What with our help, what with the absent king,
50   What with the injuries of a wanton time,
51   The seeming sufferances that you had borne,
52   And the contrarious winds that held the king
      So long in his unlucky Irish wars
      That all in England did repute him dead –
      And from this swarm of fair advantages
56   You took occasion to be quickly wooed
57   To grip the general sway into your hand;
      Forgot your oath to us at Doncaster;
      And, being fed by us, you used us so
60   As that ungentle gull, the cuckoo's bird,

---

31 *house* family   32 *remember* remind   34 *staff of office* i.e., the sign of his position   35 *posted* rode swiftly   37 *place* position; *account* accounting, reckoning   40 *outdare* defy   43 *purpose* intend   44 *new-fallen* recently inherited (from his father, John of Gaunt)   50 *wanton* disordered, lawless   51 *sufferances* distresses, injuries   52 *contrarious* adverse   56 *occasion* opportunity   57 *grip* seize; *general sway* i.e., the populace   60 *ungentle* non-noble; *gull* nestling; *cuckoo* (a bird that lays its eggs in other birds' nests)

Useth the sparrow – did oppress our nest;
Grew by our feeding to so great a bulk
That even our love durst not come near your sight
For fear of swallowing; but with nimble wing   64
We were enforced for safety sake to fly
Out of your sight and raise this present head;   66
Whereby we stand opposèd by such means   67
As you yourself have forged against yourself
By unkind usage, dangerous countenance,   69
And violation of all faith and troth   70
Sworn to us in your younger enterprise.   71

KING

These things, indeed, you have articulate,   72
Proclaimed at market crosses, read in churches,   73
To face the garment of rebellion   74
With some fine color that may please the eye   75
Of fickle changelings and poor discontents,   76
Which gape and rub the elbow at the news   77
Of hurlyburly innovation.
And never yet did insurrection want
Such water colors to impaint his cause,   80
Nor moody beggars, starving for a time   81
Of pell-mell havoc and confusion.

PRINCE

In both your armies there is many a soul   83
Shall pay full dearly for this encounter,
If once they join in trial. Tell your nephew
The Prince of Wales doth join with all the world
In praise of Henry Percy. By my hopes,

---

64 *swallowing* i.e., being swallowed   66 *head* army   67 *means* causes, factors
69 *usage* treatment; *countenance* demeanor, behavior   70 *troth* truth   71
younger earlier, previous   72 *articulate* specified   73 *market crosses* crossways
(or centers) or markets   74 *face* trim, line   75 *color* camouflage, excuse   76
changelings turncoats, traitors; *discontents* discontented persons   77 *gape*
open their mouths (in anticipation); *rub the elbow* hug themselves (in delight)   80 *water colors* thin pretexts   81 *moody* angry, restless; *starving* eager
(but also literally hungry)   83 *your* your and ours

88 This present enterprise set off his head,
    I do not think a braver gentleman,
90 More active-valiant or more valiant-young,
    More daring or more bold, is now alive
92 To grace this latter age with noble deeds.
    For my part, I may speak it to my shame,
94 I have a truant been to chivalry;
95 And so I hear he doth account me too.
96 Yet this before my father's majesty –
    I am content that he shall take the odds
98 Of his great name and estimation,
    And will, to save the blood on either side,
100 Try fortune with him in a single fight.

KING

101 And, Prince of Wales, so dare we venture thee,
102 Albeit considerations infinite
103 Do make against it. No, good Worcester, no!
    We love our people well; even those we love
    That are misled upon your cousin's part;
    And, will they take the offer of our grace,
    Both he, and they, and you, yea, every man
    Shall be my friend again, and I'll be his.
    So tell your cousin, and bring men word
110 What he will do. But if he will not yield,
111 Rebuke and dread correction wait on us,
    And they shall do their office. So be gone.
    We will not now be troubled with reply.
    We offer fair; take it advisedly.

                              Exit Worcester [with Vernon].

PRINCE

    It will not be accepted, on my life.
    The Douglas and the Hotspur both together
    Are confident against the world in arms.

---

88 *off his head* discounted, not held against him   **92** *latter* present   **94** *truant* traitor, deserter   **95** *account* esteem   **96** *this before* i.e., sworn by   **98** *estimation* reputation   **101** *dare* would dare; *venture* risk, gamble   **102** *Albeit* were it not that   **103** *make* argue, determine   **111** *wait on us* are in attendance upon us

KING
> Hence, therefore, every leader to his charge;
> For, on their answer, will we set on them,
> And God befriend us as our cause is just.   *120*

> > *Exeunt. Prince, Falstaff [remain].*

FALSTAFF   Hal, if thou see me down in the battle and be-
stride me, so! 'Tis a point of friendship.   *122*

PRINCE   Nothing but a colossus can do thee that friend-   *123*
ship. Say thy prayers, and farewell.

FALSTAFF   I would 'twere bedtime, Hal, and all well.

PRINCE   Why, thou owest God a death.   *[Exit.]*   *126*

FALSTAFF   'Tis not due yet: I would be loath to pay him   *127*
before his day. What need I be so forward with him   *128*
that calls not on me? Well, 'tis no matter; honor pricks   *129*
me on. Yea, but how if honor prick me off when I come   *130*
on? How then? Can honor set to a leg? No. Or an arm?   *131*
No. Or take away the grief of a wound? No. Honor
hath no skill in surgery then? No. What is honor? A   *133*
word. What is that word honor? Air – a trim reckon-   *134*
ing! Who hath it? He that died a Wednesday. Doth he
feel it? No. Doth he hear it? No. 'Tis insensible then?   *136*
Yea, to the dead. But will it not live with the living? No.
Why? Detraction will not suffer it. Therefore I'll none   *138*
of it. Honor is a mere scutcheon – and so ends my cat-   *139*
echism.   *Exit.*   *140*

✳

---

122 *so* good; *point* aspect   123 *colossus* giant   126 *death* (with pun on
"debt")   127 *loath* reluctant   128 *forward* eager   129 *pricks* urges   130
prick me off mark me (pick me) off for death   131 *set to* set   133 *surgery*
medicine   134–35 *trim reckoning* slender amount (slim thing)   136 *insen-*
sible unable to be sensed   138 *Detraction* slander   139 *scutcheon* coat of
arms borne at a funeral   139–40 *catechism* a question-and-answer rehearsal
of the principles of faith

∾ **V.2** *Enter Worcester and Sir Richard Vernon.*

WORCESTER
    O no, my nephew must not know, Sir Richard,
2   The liberal and kind offer of the king.
VERNON
    'Twere best he did.
WORCESTER   Then are we all undone.
    It is not possible, it cannot be,
    The king should keep his word in loving us.
6   He will suspect us still and find a time
    To punish this offense in other faults.
8   Supposition all our lives shall be stuck full of eyes;
    For treason is but trusted like the fox,
10   Who, ne'er so tame, so cherished and locked up,
11   Will have a wild trick of his ancestors.
12   Look how we can, or sad or merrily,
13   Interpretation will misquote our looks,
    And we shall feed like oxen at a stall,
15   The better cherished still the nearer death.
    My nephew's trespass may be well forgot;
    It hath the excuse of youth and heat of blood,
18   And an adopted name of privilege –
19   A harebrained Hotspur, governed by a spleen.
20   All his offenses live upon my head
21   And on his father's. We did train him on;
22   And, his corruption being ta'en from us,
23   We, as the spring of all, shall pay for all.
    Therefore, good cousin, let not Harry know,
    In any case, the offer of the king.
    Enter Hotspur [and Douglas].

V.2 Shrewsbury battlefield, the rebel camp   **2** *liberal* generous   **6** *still* constantly   **8** *Supposition* suspicion; *stuck full of* have many   **10** *ne'er so* be he never so   **11** *wild trick* trait   **12** *Look* behave   **13** *misquote* misreport, misconstrue   **15** *cherished* fed   **18** *adopted name of privilege* i.e., a nickname   **19** *spleen* fiery temper   **20–21** *All . . . father's* his father and I will be held responsible for his offenses   **21** *train* lure   **22** *corruption* guilt; *being ta'en* being derived   **23** *spring* source

VERNON
 Deliver what you will, I'll say 'tis so.
 Here comes your cousin.
HOTSPUR   My uncle is returned.
 Deliver up my Lord of Westmoreland.   28
 Uncle, what news?
WORCESTER
 The king will bid you battle presently.   30
DOUGLAS
 Defy him by the Lord of Westmoreland.   31
HOTSPUR
 Lord Douglas, go you and tell him so.
DOUGLAS
 Marry, and shall, and very willingly.   *Exit.* 33
WORCESTER
 There is no seeming mercy in the king.
HOTSPUR
 Did you beg any? God forbid!
WORCESTER
 I told him gently of our grievances,
 Of his oath-breaking, which he mended thus, 37
 By now forswearing that he is forsworn.   38
 He calls us rebels, traitors, and will scourge 39
 With haughty arms this hateful name in us. 40
  Enter Douglas.
DOUGLAS
 Arm, gentlemen! to arms! for I have thrown
 A brave defiance in King Henry's teeth,   42
 And Westmoreland, that was engaged, did bear it; 43
 Which cannot choose but bring him quickly on. 44
WORCESTER
 The Prince of Wales stepped forth before the king
 And, nephew, challenged you to single fight.

---

28 *Deliver up* release (as a hostage)   **31** *Defy him* send back your defiance
with   **33** *Marry* indeed; *and shall* and I shall   **37** *mended* excused, made up
for   **38** *forswearing* denying; *is forsworn* broke a promise   **39** *scourge* (1)
cleanse, (2) brand   **42** *brave* proud   **43** *engaged* held hostage; *bear* carry
44 *choose* help

HOTSPUR

    O, would the quarrel lay upon our heads,

    And that no man might draw short breath today

    But I and Harry Monmouth! Tell me, tell me,

50   How showed his tasking? Seemed it in contempt?

VERNON

    No, by my soul. I never in my life

    Did hear a challenge urged more modestly,

    Unless a brother should a brother dare

54   To gentle exercise and proof of arms.

55   He gave you all the duties of a man;

56   Trimmed up your praises with a princely tongue;

57   Spoke your deservings like a chronicle;

    Making you ever better than his praise

59   By still dispraising praise valued with you;

60   And, which became him like a prince indeed,

61   He made a blushing cital of himself,

    And chid his truant youth with such a grace

    As if he mastered there a double spirit

64   Of teaching and of learning instantly.

    There did he pause; but let me tell the world,

66   If he outlive the envy of this day,

67   England did never owe so sweet a hope,

68   So much misconstrued in his wantonness.

HOTSPUR

69   Cousin, I think thou art enamorèd

70   Upon his follies. Never did I hear

71   Of any prince so wild a liberty.

72   But be he as he will, yet once ere night

    I will embrace him with a soldier's arm,

74   That he shall shrink under my courtesy.

    Arm, arm with speed! and, fellows, soldiers, friends,

---

50 *tasking* challenge   54 *proof* test   55 *duties* due merits   56 *Trimmed* adorned   57 *chronicle* historical record   59 *dispraising* disparaging; *valued* compared   61 *cital* citation, account   64 *instantly* at once, simultaneously   66 *envy* hostility   67 *owe* own   68 *misconstrued* misjudged; *wantonness* sportiveness   69–70 *enamorèd / Upon* in love with   71 *liberty* licentiousness   72 *ere night* before nightfall   74 *under* from; *courtesy* (said ironically)

Better consider what you have to do   76
Than I, that have not well the gift of tongue,
Can lift your blood up with persuasion.   78
 Enter a Messenger.

MESSENGER
My lord, here are letters for you.

HOTSPUR
I cannot read them now. –   80
O gentlemen, the time of life is short!
To spend that shortness basely were too long   82
If life did ride upon a dial's point,   83
Still ending at the arrival of an hour.   84
An if we live, we live to tread on kings;   85
If die, brave death, when princes die with us!   86
Now for our consciences, the arms are fair,   87
When the intent of bearing them is just.
 Enter another Messenger.

MESSENGER
My lord, prepare. The king comes on apace.   89

HOTSPUR
I thank him that he cuts me from my tale,   90
For I profess not talking. Only this –   91
Let each man do his best; and here draw I
A sword whose temper I intend to stain   93
With the best blood that I can meet withal
In the adventure of this perilous day.
Now, Esperance! Percy! and set on.   96
Sound all the lofty instruments of war,
And by that music let us all embrace;
For, heaven to earth, some of us never shall   99

---

76 *Better consider* you can better consider   78 *Can . . . persuasion* can inspire
you   82 *basely* in a low manner, ignobly   83 *dial's* clock's   84 *Still . . . hour*
if life were only an hour long   85 *An* even; *tread on* tread as   86 *brave* glorious   87 *Now for* now, as for   89 *apace* quickly   90 *cuts me* cuts me short
91 *profess not* am no good at, don't claim to be (a talker)   93 *temper* steel
96 *Esperance* hope (the Percy family battle cry)   99 *heaven to earth* heaven
bet against earth

100   A second time do such a courtesy.
     Here they embrace. The trumpets sound. [Exeunt.]

                        *

∽ **V.3** *The King enters with his power. Alarum to the
battle. [Exeunt.] Then enter Douglas and Sir Walter
Blunt.*

BLUNT
    What is thy name, that in battle thus
    Thou crossest me? What honor dost thou seek
3   Upon my head?
DOUGLAS   Know then my name is Douglas,
    And I do haunt thee in the battle thus
5   Because some tell me that thou art a king.
BLUNT
    They tell thee true.
DOUGLAS
7   The Lord of Stafford dear today hath bought
8   Thy likeness, for instead of thee, King Harry,
9   This sword hath ended him. So shall it thee,
10   Unless thou yield thee as my prisoner.
BLUNT
    I was not born a yielder, thou proud Scot;
    And thou shalt find a king that will revenge
    Lord Stafford's death.
     They fight. Douglas kills Blunt. Then enter Hotspur.
HOTSPUR O Douglas, hadst thou fought at Holmedon
    thus, I never had triumphed upon a Scot.
DOUGLAS
    All's done, all's won. Here breathless lies the king.
HOTSPUR Where?
DOUGLAS Here.

V.3 The battlefield **s.d.** *power* army; *Alarum* trumpet **3** *Upon* from **5** *a
king* (several persons were disguised as the king in order to serve as decoys)
7 *dear* dearly **8** *likeness* resemblance **9** *ended* finished, killed

HOTSPUR

   This, Douglas? No. I know this face full well.

   A gallant knight he was, his name was Blunt;   *20*

   Semblably furnished like the king himself.   *21*

DOUGLAS

   A fool go with thy soul, whither it goes!   *22*

   A borrowed title hast thou bought too dear:

   Why didst thou tell me that thou wert a king?

HOTSPUR

   The king hath many marching in his coats.   *25*

DOUGLAS

   Now, by my sword, I will kill all his coats;

   I'll murder all his wardrobe, piece by piece,

   Until I meet the king.

HOTSPUR   Up and away!

Our soldiers stand full fairly for the day.   *Exeunt.* *29*

   Alarum. Enter Falstaff [alone].

FALSTAFF   Though I could scape shot-free at London, I   *30*

fear the shot here. Here's no scoring but upon the pate.   *31*

Soft! who are you? Sir Walter Blunt. There's honor for   *32*

you! Here's no vanity! I am as hot as molten lead, and as   *33*

heavy too. God keep lead out of me. I need no more

weight than mine own bowels. I have led my rag-of-

muffins where they are peppered. There's not three of   *36*

my hundred and fifty left alive, and they are for the

town's end, to beg during life. But who comes here?   *38*

   Enter the Prince.

PRINCE

   What, stand'st thou idle here? Lend me thy sword.

   Many a nobleman lies stark and stiff   *40*

---

21 *Semblably furnished* similarly equipped, dressed   22 *A fool . . . soul* may
the name of fool go with your soul   25 *coats* vests worn over armor that display identifying coats of arms   29 *fairly* in a good position   30 *shot-free* un-
wounded, without paying bills   31 *shot* ammunition; *scoring* (1) cutting, (2)
tallying of expenses incurred; *pate* head   32 *Soft!* hark, wait   33 *Here's no
vanity* (if this isn't a good demonstration of honor's emptiness, then I don't
know what is)   36 *peppered* i.e., with shot   38 *town's end* city gate

41   Under the hoofs of vaunting enemies,
      Whose deaths are yet unrevenged. I prithee
      Lend me thy sword.

FALSTAFF   O Hal, I prithee give me leave to breathe
45   awhile. Turk Gregory never did such deeds in arms as I
46   have done this day. I have paid Percy; I have made him
      sure.

PRINCE
      He is indeed, and living to kill thee.
      I prithee lend me thy sword.

50 FALSTAFF   Nay, before God, Hal, if Percy be alive, thou
      get'st not my sword; but take my pistol, if thou wilt.

52 PRINCE   Give it me. What, is it in the case?

53 FALSTAFF   Ay, Hal. 'Tis hot, 'tis hot. There's that will sack
      a city.

      The Prince draws it out and finds it to be a bottle of sack.

PRINCE
      What, is it a time to jest and dally now?
      He throws the bottle at him.   *Exit.*

56 FALSTAFF   Well, if Percy be alive, I'll pierce him. If he do
      come in my way, so; if he do not, if I come in his will-
58   ingly, let him make a carbonado of me. I like not such
      grinning honor as Sir Walter hath. Give me life; which
60   if I can save, so; if not, honor comes unlooked for, and
      there's an end.   *Exit.*

*

---

41 *vaunting* vanquishing, triumphant   45 *Turk Gregory* (Turk is a term for a tyrant; Gregory refers either to Pope Gregory VII, who was renowned for violence, or Gregory XIII [1572–85], enemy of England and instigator of the Saint Bartholomew's Day massacre in France in 1572)   46 *paid* put paid to, finished off   46–47 *made him sure* made certain of his death   52 *case* holster   53 *hot* i.e., after much firing   56 *Percy* (pronounced "Perce")   58 *carbonado* scored steak for broiling   60 *so* well enough

✷ **V.4** *Alarum. Excursions. Enter the King, the Prince,
Lord John of Lancaster, Earl of Westmoreland.*

KING
 I prithee, Harry, withdraw thyself; thou bleedest too
   much.
 Lord John of Lancaster, go you with him.
JOHN
 Not I, my lord, unless I did bleed too.
PRINCE
 I do beseech your majesty make up,   4
 Lest your retirement do amaze your friends.   5
KING
 I will do so.
 My Lord of Westmoreland, lead him to his tent.
WESTMORELAND
 Come, my lord, I'll lead you to your tent.
PRINCE
 Lead me, my lord? I do not need your help;
 And God forbid a shallow scratch should drive   10
 The Prince of Wales from such a field as this,
 Where stained nobility lies trodden on,
 And rebels' arms triumph in massacres!
JOHN
 We breathe too long. Come, cousin Westmorland,   14
 Our duty this way lies. For God's sake, come.
               [Exeunt Prince John and Westmoreland.]
PRINCE
 By God, thou hast deceived me, Lancaster!   16
 I did not think thee lord of such a spirit.
 Before, I loved thee as a brother, John;
 But now, I do respect thee as my soul.

V.4 s.d. *Excursions* sorties **4** *make up* advance **5** *retirement* retreat; *amaze*
alarm; *friends* allies, forces **14** *breathe* pause to catch breath **16** *Lancaster*
i.e., his brother John

KING

20 I saw him hold Lord Percy at the point
21 With lustier maintenance than I did look for
    Of such an ungrown warrior.

PRINCE   O, this boy
    Lends mettle to us all!   *Exit.*
    [Enter Douglas.]

DOUGLAS

24 Another king? They grow like Hydra's heads.
    I am the Douglas, fatal to all those
    That wear those colors on them. What art thou
    That counterfeit'st the person of a king?

KING

    The king himself, who, Douglas, grieves at heart
29 So many of his shadows thou hast met,
30 And not the very king. I have two boys
31 Seek Percy and thyself about the field;
32 But, seeing thou fall'st on me so luckily,
33 I will assay thee. So defend thyself.

DOUGLAS

    I fear thou art another counterfeit;
    And yet, in faith, thou bearest thee like a king.
    But mine I am sure thou art, whoe'er thou be,
    And thus I win thee.
        They fight. The King being in danger, enter Prince of
        Wales.

PRINCE

38 Hold up thy head, vile Scot, or thou art like
    Never to hold it up again. The spirits
40 Of valiant Shirley, Stafford, Blunt are in my arms.
    It is the Prince of Wales that threatens thee,
    Who never promiseth but he means to pay.
        They fight. Douglas flieth.

---

20 *point* i.e., of his sword   21 *lustier maintenance* energetic bearing   24
Hydra's heads (the heads of the monster Hydra grew again, two for one, as fast
as they were cut off)   29 *So many* that so many; *shadows* likeness   31 *Seek*
seeking   32 *fall'st on* come upon   33 *assay* challenge thee   38 *like* likely

Cheerly, my lord. How fares your grace?   43
Sir Nicholas Gawsey hath for succor sent,   44
And so hath Clifton. I'll to Clifton straight.   45

KING
Stay and breathe awhile.
Thou hast redeemed thy lost opinion,   47
And showed thou mak'st some tender of my life,   48
In this fair rescue thou hast brought to me.

PRINCE
O God, they did me too much injury   50
That ever said I hearkened for your death.   51
If it were so, I might have let alone
The insulting hand of Douglas over you,   53
Which would have been as speedy in your end
As all the poisonous potions in the world,
And saved the treacherous labor of your son.

KING
Make up to Clifton; I'll to Sir Nicholas Gawsey.   *Exit.* 57
    Enter Hotspur.

HOTSPUR
If I mistake not, thou art Harry Monmouth.

PRINCE
Thou speak'st as if I would deny my name.

HOTSPUR
My name is Harry Percy.   60

PRINCE   Why, then I see
A very valiant rebel of the name.
I am the Prince of Wales, and think not, Percy,
To share with me in glory any more.
Two stars keep not their motion in one sphere,   64
Nor can one England brook a double reign   65
Of Harry Percy and the Prince of Wales.

---

43 *Cheerly* look cheerfully   44 *succor* aid, help   45 *straight* straightaway
47 *opinion* reputation   48 *tender* regard   51 *hearkened* listened, waited   53
insulting exulting, demeaning   57 *Make up* advance to   64 *sphere* orbit   65
brook tolerate

HOTSPUR

> Nor shall it, Harry, for the hour is come
> To end the one of us; and would to God
> Thy name in arms were now as great as mine!

PRINCE

70   I'll make it greater ere I part from thee,
71   And all the budding honors on thy crest
72   I'll crop to make a garland for my head.

HOTSPUR

73   I can no longer brook thy vanities.
> *They fight. Enter Falstaff.*

FALSTAFF   Well said, Hal! to it, Hal! Nay, you shall find
no boy's play here, I can tell you.
> *Enter Douglas. He fighteth with Falstaff, who falls*
> *down as if he were dead. [Exit Douglas.] The Prince*
> *killeth Percy.*

HOTSPUR

> O Harry, thou hast robbed me of my youth!
> I better brook the loss of brittle life
> Than those proud titles thou hast won of me.
> They wound my thoughts worse than thy sword in flesh.
80   But thoughts the slaves of life, and life time's fool,
81   And time, that takes survey of all the world,
> Must have a stop. O, I could prophesy,
> But that the earthy and cold hand of death
> Lies on my tongue. No, Percy, thou art dust,
> And food for –
> *[Dies.]*

PRINCE

> For worms, brave Percy. Fare thee well, great heart.
> Ill-weaved ambition, how much art thou shrunk!
> When that this body did contain a spirit,
89   A kingdom for it was too small a bound;
90   But now two paces of the vilest earth
> Is room enough. This earth that bears thee dead

---

71 *crest* helmet   72 *crop* pluck   73 *vanities* boasts   80 *thoughts the* thoughts
that are; *fool* plaything   81 *takes survey* oversees   89 *bound* territory, limit

Bears not alive so stout a gentleman.   92
If thou wert sensible of courtesy,   93
I should not make so dear a show of zeal.   94
But let my favors hide thy mangled face;   95
And, even in thy behalf, I'll thank myself
For doing these fair rites of tenderness.
Adieu, and take thy praise with thee to heaven.
Thy ignominy sleep with thee in the grave,
But not remembered in thy epitaph.   100
  He spieth Falstaff on the ground.
What, old acquaintance? Could not all this flesh
Keep in a little life? Poor Jack, farewell!
I could have better spared a better man.
O, I should have a heavy miss of thee   104
If I were much in love with vanity.   105
Death hath not struck so fat a deer today,
Though many dearer, in this bloody fray.
Emboweled will I see thee by-and-by;   108
Till then in blood by noble Percy lie.   *Exit.*
  Falstaff riseth up.
FALSTAFF   Emboweled? If thou embowel me today, I'll   110
give you leave to powder me and eat me too tomorrow.   111
'Sblood, 'twas time to counterfeit, or that hot terma- 112
gant Scot had paid me scot and lot too. Counterfeit? I 113
lie; I am no counterfeit. To die is to be a counterfeit, for
he is but the counterfeit of a man who hath not the life
of a man; but to counterfeit dying when a man thereby
liveth, is to be no counterfeit, but the true and perfect
image of life indeed. The better part of valor is discre- 118
tion, in the which better part I have saved my life.
Zounds, I am afraid of this gunpowder Percy, though   120
he be dead. How if he should counterfeit too, and rise?

---

92 *stout* brave, valiant   93 *sensible of* able to sense   94 *so . . . zeal* so enthusiastic a demonstration of admiration   95 *favors* plumes, scarf   104 *heavy* (1) severe, (2) weighty   105 *vanity* frivolity   108 *Emboweled* eviscerated, preparatory to embalming a corpse   111 *powder* pickle in salt   112–13 *termagant* violent   113 *paid* i.e., killed; *scot and lot* thoroughly   118 *part* quality, role

By my faith, I am afraid he would prove the better
counterfeit. Therefore I'll make him sure; yea, and I'll
swear I killed him. Why may not he rise as well as I?
125 Nothing confutes me but eyes, and nobody sees me.
Therefore, sirrah, *[Stabs him.]* with a new wound in
your thigh, come you along with me.
   He takes up Hotspur on his back. Enter Prince, and
   John of Lancaster.

PRINCE
128 Come, brother John; full bravely hast thou fleshed
129 Thy maiden sword.

JOHN   But, soft! whom have we here?
130 Did you not tell me this fat man was dead?

PRINCE
   I did; I saw him dead,
   Breathless and bleeding on the ground. Art thou alive?
133 Or is it fantasy that plays upon our eyesight?
   I prithee speak. We will not trust our eyes
   Without our ears. Thou art not what thou seem'st.

136 FALSTAFF   No, that's certain, I am not a double man; but
137 if I be not Jack Falstaff, then am I a jack. There is Percy.
   If your father will do me any honor, so; if not, let him
   kill the next Percy himself. I look to be either earl or
140 duke, I can assure you.

PRINCE   Why, Percy I killed myself, and saw thee dead!

FALSTAFF   Didst thou? Lord, Lord, how this world is
   given to lying. I grant you I was down, and out of
   breath, and so was he; but we rose both at an instant
   and fought a long hour by Shrewsbury clock. If I may
   be believed, so; if not, let them that should reward valor
   bear the sin upon their own heads. I'll take it upon my
   death, I gave him this wound in the thigh. If the man
   were alive and would deny it, zounds! I would make
150 him eat a piece of my sword.

---

125 *confutes . . . eyes* stops me but an eyewitness   128 *fleshed* initiated   129
maiden virgin   133 *fantasy* hallucination   136 *double man* (1) ghost, (2)
two men   137 *jack* knave

JOHN
    This is the strangest tale that ever I heard.
PRINCE
    This is the strangest fellow, brother John.
    Come, bring your luggage nobly on your back.
    For my part, if a lie may do thee grace,   154
    I'll gild it with the happiest terms I have.
        A retreat is sounded.
    The trumpet sounds retreat; the day is ours.
    Come, brother, let's to the highest of the field,
    To see what friends are living, who are dead.
                Exeunt [Prince Henry and Prince John].
FALSTAFF   I'll follow, as they say, for reward. He that re-
    wards me, God reward him. If I do grow great, I'll grow   160
    less; for I'll purge, and leave sack, and live cleanly, as a 161
    nobleman should do.   *Exit [bearing off the body].*

                        *

∾ **V.5** *The trumpets sound. Enter the King, Prince of
    Wales, Lord John of Lancaster, Earl of Westmoreland,
    with Worcester and Vernon prisoners.*

KING
    Thus ever did rebellion find rebuke.
    Ill-spirited Worcester, did not we send grace,   2
    Pardon, and terms of love to all of you?
    And wouldst thou turn our offers contrary?   4
    Misuse the tenor of thy kinsman's trust?   5
    Three knights upon our party slain today,
    A noble earl, and many a creature else
    Had been alive this hour,
    If like a Christian thou hadst truly borne
    Betwixt our armies true intelligence.   10

---

154 *grace* credit   160 *great* i.e., in status, size, or funds   161 *purge* (1) diet,
with laxatives, (2) repent
    V.5 The king's command post   2 *grace* mercy   4 *contrary* away   5
Misuse . . . trust abuse Hotspur's trust by concealing my offer of mercy from
him   10 *intelligence* report

WORCESTER
 What I have done my safety urged me to;
 And I embrace this fortune patiently,
 Since not to be avoided it falls on me.

KING
 Bear Worcester to the death, and Vernon too;
15 Other offenders we will pause upon.
      [Exeunt Worcester and Vernon, guarded.]
 How goes the field?

PRINCE
 The noble Scot, Lord Douglas, when he saw
 The fortune of the day quite turned from him,
 The noble Percy slain, and all his men
20 Upon the foot of fear, fled with the rest;
 And falling from a hill, he was so bruised
 That the pursuers took him. At my tent
 The Douglas is, and I beseech your grace
 I may dispose of him.

KING   With all my heart.

PRINCE
 Then, brother John of Lancaster, to you
26 This honorable bounty shall belong.
27 Go to the Douglas and deliver him
 Up to his pleasure, ransomless and free.
 His valors shown upon our crests today
30 Have taught us how to cherish such high deeds,
 Even in the bosom of our adversaries.

JOHN
 I thank your grace for this high courtesy,
 Which I shall give away immediately.

KING
 Then this remains, that we divide our power.
 You, son John, and my cousin Westmoreland,
36 Towards York shall bend you with your dearest speed
 To meet Northumberland and the prelate Scroop,

---

15 *pause* wait 20 *Upon the foot of fear* in flight for fear 26 *bounty* act of
benevolence 27 *deliver* free 36 *bend* direct

Who, as we hear, are busily in arms.
Myself and you, son Harry, will towards Wales
To fight with Glendower and the Earl of March.   *40*
Rebellion in this land shall lose his sway,
Meeting the check of such another day;
And since this business so fair is done,
Let us not leave till all our own be won.   *Exeunt.* 44

---

44 *leave* cease

FOR THE BEST IN PAPERBACKS, LOOK FOR THE

The distinguished Pelican Shakespeare series, newly revised
to be the premier choice for students, professors, and
general readers well into the 21st century

Antony and Cleopatra
ISBN 0-14-071452-9

The Comedy of Errors
ISBN 0-14-071474-X

Coriolanus
ISBN 0-14-071473-1

Cymbeline
ISBN 0-14-071472-3

Henry IV, Part I
ISBN 0-14-071456-1

Henry IV, Part 2
ISBN 0-14-071457-X

Henry V
ISBN 0-14-071458-8

King Lear
ISBN 0-14-071476-6

King Lear (The Quarto and Folio Texts)
ISBN 0-14-071490-1

Macbeth
ISBN 0-14-071478-2

Much Ado About Nothing
ISBN 0-14-071480-4

The Narrative Poems
ISBN 0-14-071481-2

Richard III
ISBN 0-14-071483-9

Romeo and Juliet
ISBN 0-14-071484-7

The Tempest
ISBN 0-14-071485-5

Timon of Athens
ISBN 0-14-071487-1

Titus Andronicus
ISBN 0-14-071491-X

Twelfth Night
ISBN 0-14-071489-8

The Two Gentlemen of Verona
ISBN 0-14-071461-8

The Winter's Tale
ISBN 0-14-071488-X

All's Well That Ends Well
ISBN 0-14-071460-X

As You Like It
ISBN 0-14-071471-5

Hamlet
ISBN 0-14-071454-5

Henry VI, Part 1
ISBN 0-14-071465-0

Henry VI, Part 2
ISBN 0-14-071466-9

Henry VI, Part 3
ISBN 0-14-071467-7

Henry VIII
ISBN 0-14-071475-8

Julius Caesar
ISBN 0-14-071468-5

King John
ISBN 0-14-071459-6

Love's Labor's Lost
ISBN 0-14-071477-4

Measure for Measure
ISBN 0-14-071479-0

The Merchant of Venice
ISBN 0-14-071462-6

The Merry Wives of Windsor
ISBN 0-14-071464-2

A Midsummer Night's Dream
ISBN 0-14-071455-3

Othello
ISBN 0-14-071463-4

Pericles
ISBN 0-14-071469-3

Richard II
ISBN 0-14-071482-0

The Sonnets
ISBN 0-14-071453-7

The Taming of the Shrew
ISBN 0-14-071451-0

Troilus and Cressida
ISBN 0-14-071486-3